THE GYPSIES

ALEXANDER PUSHKIN

THE GYPSIES

& OTHER NARRATIVE POEMS

Translated with an introduction and notes by

ANTONY WOOD

Engravings by Simon Brett

Angel Classics
London

First published in Great Britain in 2006 by
Angel Books, 3 Kelross Road, London N5 2QS
Reissued in Angel Classics, 2013

Drawing by Pushkin reproduced on page xxxviii
by permission of the Institute of Russian Literature,
Russian Academy of Sciences, St. Petersburg.

A CIP catalogue record for this book is available
from the British Library

ISBN-13: 978-0-946162-84-0

Printed in the United States of America

To the memory of my father
with his precise sense of language
and of everything else

CONTENTS

ACKNOWLEDGMENTS

I should like to thank Mark Cohen, Mary Flannery, Peter France, John Fuller, Alla Gelich, James Greene, the late Bernard Johnson, Yuri Kleiner, Christopher Logue, Stanley Mitchell, and Delia Preiss for their comments on work in progress; and Angela Livingstone, who read successive drafts and with whom much was discussed. To my wife Hazel I owe more than I can say for her continuous scrutiny and robust comments.

I had long been trying to think of a way of getting my brother-in-law Simon Brett to collaborate on a book project, and a happy coincidence between the present publisher and the two of us at last made this a reality. I hope that his vigorous engravings might play their part towards getting Pushkin more generally seen in the broader European cultural context in which he truly belongs.

A. W.

the comic poem *Count Nulin*, is contained in this selection; it might be described as a sport springing from *Eugene Onegin*. After this, Pushkin wrote no finer narrative poem in this category until his crowning masterpiece *The Bronze Horseman*, which in my opinion no translator should attempt who doesn't approach the task as the high-point of a life's work.

The Tale of the Dead Princess and the Seven Champions is a splendid example of folk tale (the *Snow White* story) turned into art, throwing into deeper relief the extraordinary originality of *The Tale of the Golden Cockerel*, in which Pushkin uses the folk-tale form to get a number of things off his chest. *The Dead Princess*, which is a good deal more than the telling of a very familiar story, is the least familiar of these five works in the English-speaking world.

Like all the other poems in this selection, *The Bridegroom,* the longest and most complex of Pushkin's ballads, has a link with the West. This is not accidental. Pushkin, drawn towards French and especially English literature throughout his life, wrote as a European as well as a Russian, and throughout this book it has been my aspiration to do him justice as both in what became his favorite literary foreign language.

There have of course been previous English versions of all these poems. This is not the place for me to comment on any of them in detail. I have, however, ventured some judgments about earlier Pushkin translations in a wider discussion of problems of translation at the end of this book. I have endeavored to make versions that work as English verse, and in a Pushkinian way, and it is my hope not only that they might be enjoyed in themselves but also that the distinctiveness of their originals might be sufficiently discernible in them to make some comparison possible between Pushkin and English poets.

This book has grown out of a smaller volume, *The Bridegroom*, published by Angel Books, London, in 2002 and containing *Count Nulin* and *The Tale of the Golden Cockerel* as well as the title poem. I am grateful to David Godine for inviting me to reshape this project on a larger scale. The extent of the original volume is more than doubled by the addition of *The Gypsies* and *The Tale of the Dead Princess*, with a corresponding expansion of the Introduction and endnotes and widening of the range of moods and stylistic levels. I have taken the opportunity of making some amendments to the original three translations, and in a new Afterword have discussed questions of translation at greater length.

ANTONY WOOD
London, 2005

INTRODUCTION

ALEXANDER PUSHKIN is central not only to Russian culture but also to Russian identity. He gave the Russians a language, a literature, and an inspirational demonstration of human claims against state power.

His verse stands out from that of his contemporaries of the Golden Age of Russian poetry – the first three decades of the nineteenth century – in three main ways. First, it makes poetry of plain, spoken language. "Instead of the high-flown language of the gods," a listener to Pushkin reading his newly written historical tragedy *Boris Godunov* reminisces, "we heard language that was simple, lucid, and everyday, and at the same time poetically enchanting!"* He popularized a new layer of words of subjective and emotional content introduced by the writer and historian Karamzin, modeled on French, such as *trogatel'nyy* ("touching") and *zanimatel'nyy* ("absorbing"), for which no equivalents had existed before in written Russian.

Second, and allied with the first point: Pushkin writes *lightly*. "Lightness," writes Andrey Sinyavsky, "is the first thing we get out of his works. . . . Before Pushkin there was almost no light verse [in Russia]

* Quoted from *Pushkin on Literature*, edited and translated by Tatiana Wolff (London, 1998), p. 180.

... and suddenly, out of the blue, there appeared curtsies and turns comparable to nothing and no one, speed, onslaught, bounciness, the ability to prance, to gallop, to take hurdles, to do splits ..."*

Third, Pushkin writes *personally*. His lyric poems constitute a kind of emotional diary throughout his life; he writes of his African blood, his boredom in the countryside, insomnia, being with his nanny – above all, the impact made on him by women.

His extensive and varied œuvre fertilized the soil for Russian literature throughout the rest of the century and remained inspirational to Russian writers in the next. His completed work includes more than eight hundred lyric poems, a dozen narrative poems, five verse folk tales, six verse plays, a novel in verse, a novel in prose, six short prose tales, a work of historiography, diaries, and reminiscences.

But Pushkin was no narrow Russian nationalist. He was steeped in West European culture from medicine to aesthetics, and much of his writing and thinking responds to Western literature and ideas, making him a powerful influence in the tug-of-war between Westernizers and Slavophiles that has gone on in Russia from his death to the present day. He believed in the value of translation, making a number of translations and adaptations himself, especially from English. "Translators," he once said, "are the post horses of civilization."

---

* Abram Tertz (Andrei Sinyavsky), *Strolls with Pushkin*, translated by C. T. Nepomnyashchy and S. I. Yastremski (New Haven and London, 1993), p. 51.

PREFACE

ALEXANDER PUSHKIN is such a many-sided writer that selections of his work in English have often ranged across the genres, including prose along with poetry, lyric along with narrative and dramatic verse. A statement of the *raison d'être* of the present volume might therefore be in order.

First, some of Pushkin's finest work is narrative verse of one kind or another, which accounts for a quarter of all his poetry aside from the novel in verse *Eugene Onegin*. Second, variety is as much a feature of his narrative poetry as of the rest of his œuvre. This selection of five poems – a tragic and a comic tale, an extended ballad, and two contrasting treatments of the folk-tale form – demonstrates five different ways of telling a story in verse. Third, none of Pushkin's verse is nearly so well known to the English-speaking world as *Eugene Onegin*. Yet every poem in this book, in the original at least, is a marvel of its kind and deserves to be far better known in English.

The Gypsies is a milestone work, displaying Pushkin's distinctive qualities to the full. After it he was to complete four (arguably five) more "narrative poems" in the strict Russian sense of the term – that is, a long or medium-length, usually non-stanzaic verse narrative that isn't a folk tale. One of these,

Alexander Sergeyevich Pushkin was born on 26 May 1799 in Moscow. On his father's side he was descended from an old boyar family that had sunk into obscurity. On his mother's side he was the great-grandson of an African, Abram Petrovich Gannibal,* who seems to have been the son of a prince and was brought to the court of Peter the Great as a boy, ultimately attaining eminence as a military engineer. Pushkin's was a neglected childhood; his pronounced African features may have reminded his mother of her bigamous father and turned her against her first son. The best times of his early years were spent in his father's extensive library of French literature, and listening to the conversation at literary evenings held at the house.

At the age of twelve Pushkin was admitted to the new Lyceum for gifted boys from cultured and noble families set up by Tsar Alexander I in a wing of his palace at Tsarskoye Tselo outside St. Petersburg. Tuition and board were free. Nearly one-sixth of all his lyric poems were written at the Lyceum, where he acquired his extraordinary fluency and ease in writing verse. He excelled at Russian and French literature and at fencing but took little interest in

* Long thought to have been from Abyssinia. The French-Benin scholar D. Gnammankou, however, has suggested that his birthplace was in Cameroon (T. Maksimova, *Komsomol'skaya Pravda*, St. Petersburg, March 28, 2003), while Hugh Barnes (*Gannibal*, London, 2005) opts for Chad. Debate continues.

other subjects, his performance in the final examinations earning him only a minor ministerial post.

After leaving school, Pushkin spent three years in St. Petersburg, to which his parents had now moved; he lived in a tiny room above their apartment on the Fontanka River. His lifestyle resembled Onegin's, though one imagines the latter as less dissipated. At a time of hardening autocracy, his reckless liberal verses would have landed him in Siberia had it not been for the efforts of high-placed friends, and he was sent to the more congenial South, first to the frontier town of Kishinev, Bessarabia, and then to Odessa. During his exile there and on his mother's estate, Mikhaylovskoye, near the old northwestern frontier town of Pskov – six years in all – he took advantage of ideal conditions in which to write, and was spared the fate of his fellows in the Decembrist uprising of 1825 – Siberian or Caucasian exile at mildest.

Nicholas I recalled Pushkin from exile some months after the death of his brother Alexander I and his own accession to the throne. During an interview in 1826, the new tsar extracted an undertaking from Pushkin not to write anything more "against the government," and, in order to avoid further difficulties, promised to be his personal censor. He soon delegated this duty, however, to his secret police chief Count Benckendorff, who was not so well disposed toward the poet. Pushkin was now the most popular literary figure in the country.

Two years after his return from exile Pushkin met the impoverished sixteen-year-old beauty Natalya

Goncharova, and he married her three years later. Natalya had no interest in literature; her passion was the ballroom. She turned the head of the tsar. At the age of thirty-five Pushkin suffered the indignity of being appointed Gentleman of the Chamber, traditionally an eighteen year old's post, which made the couple's attendance at court balls obligatory.

Natalya met an immigrant Frenchman, a guards officer in Russian service, Baron Georges d'Anthès. She flirted with him, and inevitably Pushkin was goaded into provoking a duel, in which he was shot in the stomach, dying two days later, on 29 January 1837, at the age of thirty-seven.

Pushkin and Natalya had four children; two of their grandchildren, a brother and a sister, married grandchildren of Nicholas I.

Most poets have only one way, at most two, of telling a story in verse. Each of the five poems in this book has its own way, and this is typical of Pushkin's experimental approach. They are placed in the order of composition: a tragic narrative poem, a ballad, a comic narrative poem, and two "folk tales," the first a purer example of the form than the second. It is generally agreed that four of these five poems show Pushkin at his best; and so too does the fifth, seriously underrated by commentators.

The Gypsies stands in the middle of the sequence of Pushkin's dozen long narrative poems. It was written in 1824, during his exile in Odessa and at Mikhaylovskoye, at the same time as he was working on the third chapter of *Onegin*. The last and most mature of the narrative poems he wrote under the impact of Byron's "eastern tales" written a decade previously, it is a showcase of Pushkinian qualities.

Toward the end of chapter 11 of Jane Austen's *Persuasion*, written at the height of Byronmania, Anne Elliot discusses the narrative poems *The Giaour* and *The Bride of Abydos* together with Scott's *Marmion* and *The Lady of the Lake* with the sensitive Captain Benwick. Learning of her interlocutor's intimate acquaintance with all Byron's "impassioned descriptions of hopeless agony," the wise Anne

> *ventured to hope he did not always read only poetry; and to say, that she thought it was the misfortune of poetry, to be seldom safely enjoyed by those who enjoyed it completely; and that the strong feelings which alone could estimate it truly, were the very feelings which ought to taste it but sparingly.*

Such thoughts could never occur to any reader of *The Gypsies*. It is like nothing else in Russian – or in English. It is as far as it is possible to get not only from "a vague something, and the dim / remoteness, and romantic roses"* of contemporary Russian elegiacs and balladry, but also from the heroic romance and exoticism of Scott and Byron, devotedly read in Russia. Pushkin pitches his poetry in everyday gypsy life. He is terse, objective, rational. His language and

---

* Pushkin, *Eugene Onegin*, II.10, translated by Vladimir Nabokov (New York and London, 1964), I, p. 134.

style are lean and uninflated, and when they are not, it is with a purpose. The term "Romantic" has caused confusion in Russia from Pushkin's day to the present. Pushkin was at heart a classical writer, and Jane Austen would surely have loved him.

While Pushkin was writing *The Gypsies*, his enthusiasm for Byron and Romanticism was vanishing, and it seems that this, together with a lingering but unfulfilled desire to deepen the poem's critique of civilization and "educated values" (see endnote to page 14, line 1), delayed publication; it appeared anonymously in 1827. (The other poems in this book first appeared more openly in journals.)

Pushkin is a highly parodic writer, often playing with genre, and especially in *The Gypsies.* For the fourth time he takes the Byronic form of the verse narrative with exotic setting,* in Byron's hands long and rambling – and confounds expectations even more than previously. The exotic becomes a central theme. Pushkin's portrayal of a primal society may be idealized, but at least it is rooted in real-life experience; on two occasions during his southern exile he had spent time with gypsies, and the seriousness with which he approached the task of writing about them is reflected in a draft preface to the poem.†

---

* After *The Prisoner of the Caucasus* and *The Robber Brothers* (1821) and *The Fountain of Bakhchisaray* (1822).

† In which he states that the gypsies of Moldavia and Bessarabia, whom he claims to have "fairly accurately described" in his poem, "are notable among other peoples for their high moral probity, being honest, for example, in commercial dealings."

The Gypsies is almost more dramatic than narrative, a story told in four different "voices": those of the narration; the urban outcast Aleko, on the run for some unspecified crime; an old gypsy; and the gypsy's daughter Zemfira. The style of each of these is distinct (though the narrative voice and the old gypsy's sometimes converge), and the characters' speeches are mostly set out under their names, as in a play text. The unfocused "Romantic" style of both Aleko's direct utterances and the narrative describing him contrast sharply, and even clash, with the beautifully in-focus narration and the personal storytelling of the old gypsy.

Eleven narrative sections, some extremely short, carry the story forward with powerful momentum, while allowing room for episodes that seem to be apart from the main story but, below the surface, aren't – such as the old gypsy's account of Ovid's exile in the area, "preserved" in folk memory since Antiquity. Exile is another of the poem's themes, very much in Pushkin's mind when he wrote it.

Pushkin makes his story out of subversion of the genre of the exotic Romantic verse tale. Aleko, in flight from the shackles of Enlightenment civilization and in search of "freedom," doesn't Romantically melt into gypsy society (neither did Ovid) and relish its free-and-easy values. His "civilized" values prove inadequate to deal with the freedom that he finds, and he responds to rivalry in love in an uncivilized way. Pushkin's treatment of the idea of freedom plays with the concepts of the Social Contract and the Noble Savage, both much in the air at the time. But his gypsies don't go in for contracts or laws; they don't limit freedom, and "punishment under the law" is seen as sinful violence. And in parodic reversal of Rousseau, Aleko, pursuing the ideal of the Noble Savage, himself comes to present the spectacle of an *ig*noble citizen.

The Gypsies has been called the first "'problem piece' . . . in Russian literature," "the first of Pushkin's 'open' masterpieces"; it does not tell a simple story or point up a single interpretation but instead poses questions for the reader to find his or her own answers to. What is freedom? What is Fate? How free are the gypsies? Is there a relationship between freedom and happiness?

It has often been pointed out that Pushkin's individual gypsy characters, despite his firsthand knowledge of them, are not real gypsies. The old man, who grows in stature in the course of the poem, is a figure of Pushkin's imagination, a good deal more than "a gypsy," while Zemfira is simply a stock type. One of the poem's early readers considered the dancing bear the only "honest" character in the poem. To Andrey Sinyavsky, the moon is the central presence (indeed, it is mentioned half a dozen times in the poem):

> *In* The Gypsies *Pushkin looked at reality from the height of the soaring moon and saw the field* (polye) – *which rhymed with "will"* (volya) *and "fate"* (dolya) – *over which, like the moon in the sky, the gypsy camp was wandering, gently rocked by an easygoing love and the most easy-*

> *going betrayal in love. These intersections of meanings, inherent in the nomadic way of life, characteristic of the female heart as well, and of the moon, and of fate, and of the camp, and of the author – endow the poem with an exceptional organicism. Everything in it seems to rotate in a single patch of light, which, however, embraces the entire universe.**

To John Bayley, the final crane image is central. Aleko, left alone in the steppe by the gypsies, is compared to a wounded crane left behind by the rest of the flock. Bayley sees Ovidian metamorphosis (Pushkin had been reading Ovid in French translation) in an ending that transforms the group of gypsies into a flock of migrating cranes.†

These responses say something about the nature of the poem that prompted them. Pushkin's work in general has been described as "kaleidoscopic" by commentators taking up the celebrated image that comes at the end of *Eugene Onegin*: "through magic crystal / I first dimly discerned / the distant outlines of a free novel" (literal translation). What brings everything together in *The Gypsies*, Pushkin's first mature extended work, is the quality of the poetry. The point was made in a celebrated exchange between Pushkin and his friend the poet Vasily Zhukovsky. "I know nothing more perfect in style

* Tertz, p. 74.

† John Bayley, *Pushkin: A Comparative Commentary* (Cambridge, 1971), p. 100.

than your *Gypsies*," the latter wrote, "but dear friend, what is its aim?" "Simply this," Pushkin replied: "the aim of poetry is poetry." Using, basically, everyday language and reference (like his gypsies', a "language poor but sonorous"), Pushkin achieves a graphic eloquence that gives memorable solidity to his created world. From a middle-distance vantage point, he brings the day-to-day life of the "migratory horde" magnificently alive, in all its "squalor and cacophony." And in debunking Romanticism, he was ahead of his time. The detailed precision with which he observes gypsy life turned out to be the beginning of "Russian Realism," the foundation for most of nineteenth-century Russian literature.

Multi-layered, cunningly structured, and daringly experimental, *The Gypsies* was the subject of much debate among Russian thinkers and critics throughout the nineteenth century and much of the twentieth, especially the old gypsy's judgment on Aleko: "Not for freedom were you born, / You want it for yourself alone...." The Byron-inspired figure of Aleko was hailed together with Eugene Onegin as an entirely new character in Russian literature, of near Hamlet-like stature, representing the played-out values of Enlightenment civilization in contrast to those of primal, innocent, rural society. The latter were identified as the values of the Russian people, as against the intellectual Enlightenment tradition of Western Europe. Dostoyevsky put Aleko and Onegin at the center of his famous "Pushkin speech" of 1880, delivered on the occasion of the unveiling of A. Opekushin's statue of Pushkin in

Moscow, considering Aleko "a stranger in his own land" and representative of the tragedy of the Russian intelligentsia cut off from the people.

To many a work by Pushkin there is an operatic footnote. *The Gypsies* is no exception. Prosper Mérimée, a great admirer of Pushkin, made a prose translation of the poem. As A. D. P. Briggs has pointed out,* both Mérimée's *Carmen* (1845), the acknowledged source for the libretto of Bizet's opera, and the opera libretto itself (1875), owe much to Pushkin's poem, which has always gone unacknowledged. The main lines of Bizet's plot, his two chief characters, Carmen and Don José, the opera's leading themes and keywords, Carmen's song "Stab me, burn me" – all this and more comes straight out of Pushkin's *Gypsies*. The title page of the opera and of every production program, Briggs argues, should in all fairness include the name of Pushkin.†

Many of Pushkin's two-dozen ballads are free translations or adaptations of foreign originals. His orig-

* "Did Carmen Come from Russia?", in the program for the English National Opera production of *Carmen*, Autumn 1995–96.

† To complete the operatic record, mention must be made of Rakhmaninov's *Aleko* (1893). Although this youthful one-act opera has not entered the repertory, it contains some pieces of striking freshness and vigor. Chaliapin made unsuccessful attempts to persuade the composer to enhance the title role by writing a second act.

inal ballad *The Bridegroom* stands fascinatingly on the convergence of three national cultures. The ballad *Lenore*, by the German Romantic poet Gottfried Bürger, published in 1774, won enormous popularity throughout Europe. Its story, based on the brief Scottish ballad *Sweet William's Ghost*, published in 1724, tells of a girl's immoderate and blasphemous grief at the death of her lover in the Seven Years' War, whose ghost appears and takes her on a nocturnal ride to his graveyard, where she falls dead. Bürger makes powerful use of the sonic resources of the German language, and of popular words such as *hopp* ("quick") and *tummle dich* ("get a move on").

William Taylor's translation of *Lenore*, which appeared in London in 1797, inspired Walter Scott's imitation of the same year. Vasily Zhukovsky, who launched the Romantic Movement in Russia in 1802 with his translation of Gray's *Elegy Written in a Country Church-Yard*, published two free versions of Bürger's ballad in 1808 and a closer translation in 1831; Pavel Katenin's version was published in 1816 and was admired by Pushkin for its wild energy. Pushkin didn't compete with these translators; instead, he composed an original ballad in the same meter (preserved in the present translation). This eight-line stanza, a combination of iambic tetrameter ("The thìrd night càme: in wìld disòrder") and trimeter ("They stìll were nòne the wìser"), is dynamic in the extreme, constantly on edge and changing rhythm; its use in this poem is unique in Pushkin.

The Bridegroom was written in 1824–25, during Pushkin's first year of exile at Mikhaylovskoye. The story of the merchant's daughter and her traumatic experience is his own, though it may be based on an oral source, perhaps told to him by the nanny of his boyhood, the serf Arina Rodionovna, in the company of whom he lived for two years at Mikhaylovskoye. It is told in the most oblique and subtle way, equally far from Bürger's head-on Romanticism and the popular balladry of Scottish and English tradition. Suspense is maintained from first stanza to last. Like other poems by Pushkin written in this period and place – the well-known lyric "Winter Evening," for example – it draws richly on popular idiom. At the same time it is full of the most sophisticated effects, from dazzling onomatopoeia – the sound of wind-tossed fir-tree tops, the escalating din of a wedding feast – to eloquent repetitions (some of these effects in the original are pointed out in the endnotes) and even occasional echoes of *Lenore*. As he often does, Pushkin has it two ways. He offers the reader the experience of a Romantic ballad, the sinister merging of dream world and reality.* But at the end, as the reader reviews what has actually happened in the story, the true nature of this highly original, once again genre-subverting and dramatic narrative emerges.

* Tatyana's dream (*Eugene Onegin*, V. 11–21, written a few months later) will be in many a reader's mind to strengthen this impression.

Count Nulin was conceived in a spirit of parody of Shakespeare's poem *The Rape of Lucrece.* "I thought," Pushkin later reminisced,

> *what if it had occurred to Lucrece to slap Tarquin's face? Maybe it would have cooled his boldness and he would have been obliged to withdraw ... Lucrece would not have stabbed herself ... Brutus would not have driven out the kings, and the world and its history would have been different.*
>
> *And so we owe the republic, the consuls, the dictators, the Catos, the Caesars, to a seduction similar to one that took place recently in our neighborhood ...**
>
> *I was struck by the idea of parodying both history and Shakespeare; I could not resist the double temptation and in two mornings had written this tale.*†

Pushkin takes the central idea in Shakespeare's poem, the rape, and mock-heroicizes it into a comic tale of rural life in his favorite meter, the iambic tetrameter. He was working on the fourth chapter of *Eugene Onegin* when he wrote *Count Nulin*, and as John Bayley has observed, "we can imagine the heroine and her husband [the small landowner and his bored young wife, hungry for social contact]

---

* Pushkin's friend Aleksey Vulf was said to have seduced the daughter of a local priest.

† Note written around 1830. Quoted from *Pushkin on Literature*, pp. 272–73.

attending Tatyana's name-day feast."* Sextus Tarquinius becomes Count Nulin, a traveling dandy who spends a jolly evening in the house of a young grass-widow and fumbles his way into her room after everyone has retired to bed. There are other playful parallels to *The Rape*:† Shakespeare's "lustful lord" becomes "our ardent hero"; Tarquin throws "his mantle rudely o'er his arm" and strikes a light with his falchion, Nulin puts on "a striped silk dressing gown" and knocks down a chair in the dark. The very name Nulin, based on the word *nul* (nil), parodies Sextus (Sixth).

But parody is not what the reader of this light-hearted poem experiences and enjoys. Uppermost is a picture of the delightful triviality of life in the country, a satirical portrait of two social types of the time, the cosmopolitan fop and the small landowner/his wife, with intimate detail of their lifestyle, material and moral. Earlier narrative poems by Pushkin belong in varying degrees – *The Gypsies*, as we have seen, only vestigially – to Romantic tradition. *Count Nulin*'s modernity of language, sensibility, and characterization found immediate response. The public loved it; reviewers found its story, despite its origins, outrageously indecent.

As so often with Pushkin, however, other concerns may lurk not far beneath the carefree surface.

---

* Bayley, p. 291.

† Those mentioned here and others are noted by A. D. P. Briggs, *Alexander Pushkin: A Critical Study* (reprinted Bristol, 1991), pp. 104–6.

His account of how he came to write *Count Nulin* continues with the cryptic sentence: "History does repeat itself strangely." In the 1920s and '30s Russian critics began to suggest that *Count Nulin* relates vitally in some way to Pushkin's serious concern with patterns of history at the time of writing (one month previously he had completed the historical tragedy *Boris Godunov*, which deals with cataclysmic historical events), and another Russian scholar has speculated that at this time "Pushkin pondered on history's laws and on the possibility of a chain of trifling accidents jeopardizing a great event."*

Early in December 1825, tucked away in Mikhaylovskoye, Pushkin heard of the death of Alexander I. Excitedly he looked forward to great changes in Russia and in his own life. He even set out illicitly for St. Petersburg, but turned back when he encountered unlucky omens – he met a priest and a hare crossed his path. On the very day he would have expected to be in St. Petersburg, he started to write *Count Nulin* instead, and finished it on the following day, when the abortive Decembrist uprising was taking place in the capital. But for the omens, he would have been there ("I would have been in the ranks of the rebels," he said to Nicholas I during the interview of 1826).

---

* Yu. M. Lotman, quoted by Boris Gasparov, "The Apocalyptic Theme in Pushkin's *Count Nulin*," in *Text and Context: Essays to Honor Nils Åke Nilsson* (Stockholm, 1987), p. 17.

Pushkin completed his five *skazki*, or folk tales in verse (Russia doesn't have fairies or fairy tales), over a period of four years comparatively late in his life. Two of them are in popular style, while the other three take more literary form, in rhymed couplets. Among the latter are the two *skazki* translated in this book.

Some years before he began to write these poems, in lone exile at Mikhaylovskoye with Arina Rodionovna, Pushkin jotted down synopses of tales she told him. He wrote to his brother Lev in November 1824:

> *Do you know how I spend my day? Before dinner [i.e., lunch] I write my memoirs . . . After dinner I go riding; in the evening I listen to folk tales – and in this way compensate for the shortcomings of my cursed education. How wonderful these tales are! Each one is a poem!*

These synopses provided part-sources for three of Pushkin's *skazki*, among them *The Tale of the Dead Princess and the Seven Champions*. But the Grimms' *Sneewittchen* (*Snow White*), which Pushkin read in French translation, was his major source for this tale, written in the late autumn of 1833 at Boldino, the estate acquired from his father in the district of Nizhny Novgorod, east of Moscow; at the same time he was writing the last and greatest of his narrative poems, *The Bronze Horseman*. In *The Dead Princess* he streamlines the Grimms' storyline in a number of ways. He limits the disguised evil stepmother's attempts to kill the princess to her single appearance with the poisoned apple and conceals (or considers it superfluous to reveal) her true identity; he gives no reason for the princess's coffin being made of glass – in his tale it just mysteriously *is* (in *Sneewittchen* the coffin is placed in the open, with the princess's beauty on display to all); and he omits the Grimms' gruesome details, such as those of the stepmother's death. As in his Russian source, the brothers are not dwarfs but *bogatyri*, the giant heroes of national folklore. On the other hand, Pushkin adds major components to the story, putting flesh and blood to the Grimms' rudimentary prince and princess (magic realism in reverse?).

He makes the prince the bridegroom at the outset, and gives him a name, Yelisey. He creates a small but striking role for the brothers' brave house dog. He adds the episode of Prince Yelisey's search for his bride. A high moral thread runs through his tale. The princess behaves more like a peasant girl than a princess, cleaning and tidying up the empty house she comes upon, lighting the fire and so on, instead of, as in the Grimms' story, taking food and drink from each of the absent brothers' table settings. And the brothers' joint declaration of love for the princess and respectful acceptance of her prior betrothal are entirely Pushkin's invention.

Pushkin's achievement in making folk material into poetry is too often taken for granted. In the letter to his brother Lev quoted above, he is looking through his "magic crystal" again, glimpsing the possibilities for poetry in his nanny's storytelling. In *The Tale of the Dead Princess* more than in either of his other two literary versions of folk tales, *Tsar Saltan* and *The Tale of the Golden Cockerel*, Pushkin achieves a direct, folk-like simplicity, an intimacy abounding in diminutives (a feature of colloquial Russian), and the poem has an equal appeal to "a child of six and the most sophisticated poetry-reader of sixty," to quote the literary historian D. S. Mirsky (actually referring to *Tsar Saltan*, but he could have said the same of *The Dead Princess*).

The tale has attracted translators' attention far less than Pushkin's other poems in this book, and the occasional critical mention of it in English tends to be unenthusiastic – perhaps because the storyline is so familiar. A leading twentieth-century Russian Pushkin editor and critic, however, considered it "the most lyrical and poetic of all Pushkin's verse folk tales ... containing passages ... that belong among the finest poetry that Pushkin ever wrote."*

The Tale of the Golden Cockerel (1834) is the last of Pushkin's verse folk tales. His source used to be

* S. M. Bondi, commentary on *The Tale of the Dead Princess* in an edition of Pushkin's complete works (Moscow, 1959–62), III, p. 529; as examples of such passages, Bondi singles out the account of the Princess's burial and the Wind's reply to Prince Yelisey.

thought, vaguely but firmly, a traditional Russian one, but in 1933 Anna Akhmatova published an article in the monthly *Zvezda* showing otherwise (which may have contributed toward making her one of Zhdanov's targets in his "anti-cosmopolitan" campaign of 1946). Akhmatova discovered that Pushkin's storyline is based on that of Washington Irving's prose narrative "The Legend of the Arabian Astrologer," contained in *Tales of the Alhambra* (1832; Pushkin read a French translation of the same year), a popular compendium of history, legend, and travelogue.

Irving's is a flat narrative about a Moorish king of Granada, a good monarch who in his old age enlists the help of a wily astrologer who makes him a talisman, a bronze warrior, to warn him of approaching foes, and then by a trick takes from him his captive queen, who has limited magic powers, and disappears, leaving the king defenseless once more. From this material Pushkin fashions a closely wrought, electrifyingly dramatic tale. He makes the talisman, a golden cockerel, the central figure, and knits the other three characters – Tsar Dadon, the astrologer, and the Queen of Shamakhan – into a dynamic, eerie relationship. He makes the tsar morally culpable, withholding the astrologer's promised reward and leading an empty-headed life of complete idleness. His astrologer is faithful and does the tsar real service. The queen's sinister aura of mystery and the supernatural dominates the second half of the narrative.

Pushkin's tale is dryly, abstractly written, almost

completely without descriptive physical detail. Its tone is lightly ironical and distanced, despite popular turns of phrase. Slight archaisms underline the general detachment. The condensed language makes the gait of this tale slower and weightier than that of *The Dead Princess*, which is in the same meter (though not in my translation). One Russian critic, finding a "'dissonance' between the literary genre and the style," writes that Pushkin is using the folk-tale form "as a mask on the face of contemporary man."*

The Tale of the Golden Cockerel was written in autumn 1834, the beginning of the terrible final period of Pushkin's life. Chained to the capital by his humiliating court appointment when he wanted to write in the country, weighed down by debt, subjected to police spying (to his disgust, even letters to his wife were opened) – during this year Pushkin became extremely morose and wrote very little. While his wife was on her family estate recovering from a miscarriage brought on, so it was thought, by excessive dancing, he asked to resign his post as Gentleman of the Chamber, but the tsar prevented him from doing so by threatening to withdraw permission for him to use the imperial archives to research his history of Peter the Great if he did. He was already disenchanted with Nicholas, who had broken his undertaking to be his personal censor.

---

* Valentin Nepomnyashchy, "A Few Words about the Tale [of the Golden Cockerel]," *Soviet Literature*, 466:I (Moscow, 1987), p. 117.

In September Pushkin went alone to his estate of Boldino. Here in previous years he had spent miraculously creative autumns, but this time he produced only *The Golden Cockerel*. It isn't hard to see a bitter caricature of Nicholas in the puffed-up Dadon, the autocrat who breaks his promises; Pushkin, in fact, twice toned down a pointed reference before submitting the manuscript to the censor (see the penultimate endnote on this poem). But in the wise eunuch-astrologer and his fate, an American scholar, Sona Hoisington, has suggested further autobiographical content.* She quotes a letter from Pushkin to his wife written in July: "I came within a hair's breadth of … quarrelling with him … If I quarrel with this one – I won't find another [tsar]." The fate of the astrologer might be interpreted as a warning to himself not to go too far with tsars – though to Soviet commentators, the tale's warning of the destructive potential of female beauty was always uppermost.†

Hoisington sees evidence of an astrologer–cockerel–Pushkin nexus in the well-known sketch

---

* S. S. Hoisington, "Pushkin's Golden Cockerel: A Critical Re-examination," in *The Golden Age of Russian Literature and Thought*, edited by Derek Offord (New York, 1992), from which quotations are made.

† Rimsky-Korsakov's opera based on Pushkin turned out to be just as politically sensitive on its completion in 1907 as the original poem had been in 1835; its satirical treatment of autocracy led to a ban on performance during the composer's lifetime.

Pushkin's ink drawing on the cover of the notebook containing the fair copy of The Tale of the Golden Cockerel.

that Pushkin made for the cover of the fair copy of *The Tale of the Golden Cockerel* (see opposite). At top right, facing the bust of Tsar Dadon, is an ambiguous grotesque – presumably representing the astrologer – with "phallic-like features who appears to be making an obscene gesture at Dadon." Pushkin refers sardonically in correspondence of this time to his role as "court jester," and this autobiographical reference might be read in the depiction, in which, further, "the strong sexual overtones associated in the poem with the cockerel are transferred to the astrologer." Along with the cockerel's comb, it might be added.

The cockerel is of course a common symbol for sexual potency, and here for creative potency. Hoisington suggests that the cockerel "is a symbol of Pushkin's masculinity, that part of himself which he felt the tsar in real life had rendered impotent," observing that in the poem, when the astrologer speaks or acts on his own account, he is called "the wise man," but when he is the object of the tsar's perception he is called "the eunuch."

A second selection of Pushkin's narrative poems of similar scope to this one could be made, and one day might be made by the present translator. In the meantime, these five poems give, I think, a fair sample of the range of his narrative verse. I hope of course too that from the translations the reader without Russian might gain an idea of the kind of poet he is. In my Afterword and in the endnotes to the poems, I have tried to provide perspective to this question by giving the reader a glimpse of some of the heights that tower before the translator of Pushkin.

A. W.

THE GYPSIES

Through Bessarabia far and wide
A noisy throng of gypsies roams.
Today their worn and tattered homes
Appear above the riverside.
Like freedom, their encampment feels
Joyful, their sleep beneath the skies
Carefree; among the wagon-wheels,
Half-covered with scant canopies,
Fires burn, with families intent
Upon their supper; on the lea
The horses graze; behind one tent
A bear lies fast asleep and free.
Life resounds on every side:
The peaceful cares of families thinking
Of next day's short and early ride,
The cries of children, women singing,
And the traveling anvil ringing.
But now the hush of slumber drops
Upon the migratory horde,
Only the horses and the dogs,
Late in the silence, can be heard.
Everywhere the fires have died;
All is tranquil, and the moon,
Wandering in the heavens alone,
Shines down upon the quiet site.
Inside his tent an old man sits,
Warmed by the lingering glow of ashes,

And doesn't sleep; instead he watches
The far expanses wrapped in mists.
Somewhere on the lonely steppe
His daughter is off wandering; she
Enjoys a life of liberty,
She will be back. But night has crept
Apace, and in a little time
The moonlight will not be so bold,
And of Zemfira, not a sign;
The old man's meager meal is cold.

But here she comes, and following her
A youth that none has seen before.
"Father," declares the girl, "I found
A guest out there, beside a mound;
I've asked him home to stay with us.
He wants to be a gypsy too;
The law is after him, he says,
But I shall be his love and true.
Aleko is his name – I know
He'll go with me wherever I go."

OLD MAN

You're welcome here to what we have.
Stay for tonight, or longer if
You wish, and share our bread and roof.
Be one of us, and live our life –

The threadbare freedom of the road.
We're off tomorrow with our load;
Choose a trade to suit your flair,
Blacksmith, singer, or the bear.

ALEKO

I'll stay with you.

ZEMFIRA

Mine he shall be:
Who will drive him away from me?
It's late . . . the crescent moon has set;
Out on the steppe you cannot see,
And sleep weighs heavy on my head . . .

Day comes. Around the silent tent
The old man takes the morning mist.
"Your night of rest is at an end . . .
Rise, children, from your couch of bliss! . . ."
The people pour forth noisily;
Tents are struck, and presently
All move off as one. Now see
The gypsies overrun the plain:
In baskets slung upon their backs
Donkeys carry children playing;

Closely following in their tracks
Men, wives, girls, brothers, all together,
Young and old; din everywhere,
Songs, the roaring of the bear,
The jingling of its iron tether,
Resplendent motley raggedness,
Children's and old men's nakedness,
The barks and howls of dogs, the play
Of bagpipes, axles under stress,
Squalor and cacophony,
But all of it so live and strong,
So foreign to our empty leisure –
So foreign to the life of pleasure,
Monotonous as prisoners' song!

The young man fixed a doleful eye
Upon the now abandoned plain;
The reason for his melancholy
He dared not fathom or explain.
Beside him was dark-eyed Zemfira,
He was the world's free citizen;
Merrily the midday sun
Shone down from heavens never clearer;
What was the sorrow that oppressed him?
What was the secret that obsessed him?

God's little bird knows neither
Labor nor unrest,
Doesn't make an effort
To build a lasting nest;
At sunrise, after sleeping
Soundly all night long,
It hears the voice of God,
Wakes, and sings its song.
After spring in its glory
Sultry summer is here –
But then comes cruel weather,
Autumn of the year:
How comfortless for man;
The bird flies off, to be,
Till spring, on warmer shores
Beyond the dark blue sea.

Like that bird without a care
He too, a migrant on the wing,
Couldn't settle anywhere,
Couldn't get used to anything.
The road to anywhere he took,
Anywhere his night's abode,
His every day, when he awoke,
He offered to the will of God;
Life's tribulations never shook
The torpor of his heart and mind.

Sometimes that distant comet, fame,
Would stir him with its magic flame,
Or nearer pleasures he might find;
Many a time the gathered thunder
Crashed above his lonely head –
Come fair or foul, still he would slumber
Careless as ever on his bed.
Innocent of human thrall
To blind and cunning destiny
He lived . . . O God, how brutally
The passions once had torn his soul
And seethed in his tormented breast!
When was it they were put to rest?
They will awaken: wait and see!

ZEMFIRA

Tell me, my love, do you not pine
For what you've chosen to renounce?

ALEKO

What is it I have left behind?

ZEMFIRA

Your fellow countrymen, and towns.

ALEKO

Oh, if you knew those cities! – where
No one is free in anything,
Where no one breathes the morning air,
The scent of meadowland in spring;
Where love is shame, and so are brains,
They barter with their liberty
And revel in idolatry,
And all they want is gold and chains!
What have I left behind? Betrayal,
The persecution of the crowd,
The prejudice of minds grown stale,
Disgrace – of which one can be proud!

ZEMFIRA

Just think of those great rooms, and those
Carpets of many colors, those
Revels and banquets, and those clothes!

ALEKO

What is the point of such enjoyments?
If there's no love, then there's no pleasure.
Those girls . . . You are without adornments
And costly clothes – but you are better!
Never, dear friend, be different! While
You share my voluntary exile,
I'll share with you my love, my leisure!

OLD MAN

You are fond of us, although you come from
A people used to wealth and ease.
But freedom doesn't always please
Those who have lived a life of comfort.
It's said that once an emperor
Banished a subject, who then came
To live with us, a southerner
(I've long forgotten his strange name).
By then he was no longer young,
Though young and gentle in his soul –
He had the wondrous gift of song,
And in his voice you heard the fall
Of waters – he was popular;
He lived beside the Danube here
And did no harm to anyone;
His tales enchanted everyone;
Little he ever understood,
He had a child's timidity,
His frame was weak, his livelihood
Hung upon strangers' charity –
When the swift river was iced over
And blizzards raged, and bitter winds,
People from all around would cover
The saintly old man with furs and skins;
The life, however, of the poor
Was one to which he couldn't take,

He wandered pale and thin as a rake;
An angry god pursued him, for
A crime, he said, was on his hands . . .
He waited for deliverance.
The unhappy man was always grieving,
Along the Danube he would roam,
Remembering his distant home,
And bitter was that old man's weeping;
Dying, he made a last request
His yearning bones be taken south,
For they could never be at rest
On alien soil, in life, in death!

ALEKO

A son of yours, and come to this,
O Rome, O city of glorious name! . . .
Singer of love, of deities,
Now can you tell me, what is fame? –
The voice of praise, an endless knell,
A sound that runs from age to age?
The tale a gypsy has to tell,
A smoke-filled tent for all his stage?

A year goes by . . . another year.
The gypsies in their peaceful throng
Wander on, and everywhere,

Wherever they settle, they belong.
Spurning the chains of civilization,
Aleko spends, as free as they,
His each and every roaming day
Without regrets or agitation.
He and his kin are still the same,
But out of mind his former days,
He has grown used to gypsy ways,
The snugness of their nightly home,
The rapture of pure idleness,
Their language, poor but sonorous.
His shelter's shaggy guest, the bear,
A vagrant from its native lair,
Roves the Moldavian villages,
Performs its clumsy dances, gnaws
Its irritating chain, and roars
Before the wary villagers;
The bent old man is not averse
To beating on the tambourine,
Aleko leads the bear and sings,
Zemfira goes about to glean
The voluntary offerings.
Night falls; the three together make
Their meal of unreaped millet grain;
Soon the old man is nodding . . . then
The tent is tranquil in the dark.

The old man warms in springtime sun
Blood already growing cold;
His daughter, with her little one,
Sings. Aleko is appalled.

ZEMFIRA

Old husband, dread husband,
Stab your wife, burn your wife:
Firm I stand – I don't fear
Fire or the knife.

I hate you, despise you,
Another I love;
He has all my heart,
I shall die for my love.

ALEKO

That's quite enough. I cannot bear
That song, wild songs are not for me.

ZEMFIRA

Oh, not for you? That's as may be,
This is a song not meant to share.

Stab your wife, burn your wife,
I shall not show him:
Old husband, dread husband,
You shall not know him.

Fresh as the spring he is,
Hot as high summer;
How young and brave he is!
Ah! how he loves me!

How I caressed him,
Deep in the night!
How we both laughed at you,
Grizzled old fright!

ALEKO

Zemfira! That's enough for me . . .

ZEMFIRA

You understand my song is true?

ALEKO

Zemfira!

ZEMFIRA

Rage at me, you're free,
The subject of my song is you.

(*Goes away singing: "Old husband . . ." etc.*)

OLD MAN

I know that song – it's long been sung,
It was composed when we were young:

On winter nights my Mariyule,
Rocking our daughter by the fire
Out on the steppes of the Kagul,
Would sing it, and would never tire.
These days, I leave the past behind –
That song will never leave my mind.

Night, and all is quiet. The moon
Adorns the azure southern sky.
Zemfira wakens the old man:
"Father! Aleko frightens me.
Look at him: he's deeply sleeping,
But listen to him groaning – weeping."

OLD MAN

You mustn't touch him. Not a sound.
The Russians say, from midnight on
A household spirit hovers round
And cramps a sleeper's breath; by dawn
That evil spirit will be gone.
Come and sit with me.

ZEMFIRA

"Zemfira!"
He whispered, father!

OLD MAN

You are his troth
Even in sleep, and you are dearer
Than all the world to him.

ZEMFIRA

I loathe
His love. How bored I am! I long
For freedom – I am already . . . No!
Not out loud . . . Do you hear him now?
Another name is on his tongue . . .

OLD MAN

Whose name!

ZEMFIRA

Just listen! How he chews
And groans! . . . It's terrible to hear it! . . .
I'll wake him.

OLD MAN

It will be no use,
You mustn't chase away the spirit –
It goes whenever the time is right . . .

ZEMFIRA

He called to me . . . he's turned his head . . .

Now he's starting from the bed –
I'll go to him – sleep now, goodnight.

ALEKO

Where have you been?

ZEMFIRA

Sitting with father.
Some spirit has been cruelly
Lashing your soul, making you suffer
While you slept; you frightened me,
Your teeth were grinding in your mouth,
You called me.

ALEKO

You were in my dream.
And it was this: I saw us both . . .
Terrible things were in my dream!

ZEMFIRA

Dreams and nightmares are deceiving.
Don't believe them.

ALEKO

I believe in
Nothing at all, not dreams, nor sweet
Assurances, not even your heart.

OLD MAN

Why do you sigh, young hothead? Here
People are free, the sky is clear,
Our women's beauty is above
All others'. Grief destroys; don't grieve.

ALEKO

Father, I have lost her love.

OLD MAN

Console yourself; she is a child.
You are downcast unreasonably:
Your love is labor, grief, and bile;
A woman loves light-heartedly.
Look at the free moon in the sky –
Her beams will shine indifferently
On nature as she passes by.
She comes to a cloud and lights it up,
Moves to another; she'll not stop.
Who shall place her in the skies
And tell her where she has to stay!
To a young girl's heart, who is to say:
Love only once, let that suffice!
Console yourself.

ALEKO

Ah, how she loved me!
And in the silence of the steppe,
When all the world was fast asleep,
How she used to lean towards me!
Full of childlike happiness,
How often she would put to flight
The melancholy of the night
With whispering or a passionate kiss!
But now Zemfira is too bold . . .
Now my Zemfira has grown cold!

OLD MAN

Listen: I will relate to you
A little of my history.
Our Danube – it was long ago –
Was not yet sailed by Mòskaly;
Sorrow, Aleko, I recall.
The Sultan held us, then, in thrall;
From the high towers of Akkerman
A pasha ruled the Budzhak plain –
In those days I was young; my soul
Was cheerful; on my head no sign
Of gray. Among the beauties, one
I admired and worshiped like the sun,
And at long last, I called her mine . . .

Ah, how soon my youth flashed by –
As swiftly as a shooting star!
But then the time of love passed by
More swiftly still: a single year
Maryula gave me, that was all.

Once we were skirting the Kagul,
And met an unknown gypsy band;
They pitched their tents alongside ours,
And on that wild and hilly ground
They spent the next two nights with us.
The third night came, and they had gone –
Maryula left her little daughter,
And me, in her hotfoot departure.
I slept in perfect peace; at dawn
My loved one was no longer there!
I searched, I called – no trace of her.
Zemfira cried and pined, and I
Wept with her – nowadays I shun
All women in the world, my eye
Will never rest with any pleasure
On female beauty, my lone leisure
Is never shared with anyone.

ALEKO

If I'd been you, I would have gone

Straight after her, my faithless wife –
Put her, her captors, to the knife.

OLD MAN

Why? Youth is freer than a bird;
You'll try to hold back love in vain;
Joy comes to everyone in turn,
And what has been won't come again.

ALEKO

I could not live like that. No foe
Deprives me of my rights – ah no!
I will at least enjoy revenge.
No! If I found my enemy
High on a cliff above the sea,
Asleep, I swear I'd never blench –
My foot would send the criminal
Over the cliff and down to the surf;
His sudden terror in the fall
Would fill me with unholy mirth –
How I should laugh to hear him howl!

YOUNG GYPSY

One more kiss . . . One more, just one . . .

ZEMFIRA

My husband has a jealous eye.

GYPSY

A longer one! . . . To say goodbye.

ZEMFIRA

Well, goodbye then – now, he'll come.

GYPSY

The next time – when will it be safe?

ZEMFIRA

When the moon goes up tonight –
There, past the mound, above the grave . . .

GYPSY

She will deceive me!

ZEMFIRA

Run and hide!
He's coming! . . . Here I am, my love.

Aleko sleeps. But in his mind
A dreadful vision is played out;

He wakes in darkness with a shout
And reaches with a jealous hand –
A hand, however, that grows shy
Clutching a cold coverlet;
His loved one is no longer by . . .
He sits up trembling on the bed . . .
Silence all around him – rent
By sudden fear, he listens, then,
Hot and cold, he leaves the tent
To wander, terrible of mien,
Around the carts; all sound has ceased,
The fields are resting in the night,
The moon has disappeared in mist,
Leaving the stars' uncertain light;
Faintly showing in the dew,
A track meanders out of view
Beyond the mounds; without delay
He follows the ill-fated way.

Far off before him in the night,
Beside the track, a grave shows white . . .
A sense of dread possesses him,
Weak and tired in every limb
On he walks . . . Then . . . a chimera?
Suddenly two shadows loom,
He hears a whispering, nearer, nearer,
Above the desecrated tomb.

FIRST VOICE

It's time to go now . . .

SECOND VOICE

No . . .

FIRST VOICE

It's time,

My love.

SECOND VOICE

No, no, stay here. Be mine

Till dawn.

FIRST VOICE

It's late.

SECOND VOICE

You love so coyly.

One minute more!

FIRST VOICE

You will destroy me.

SECOND VOICE

One minute!

FIRST VOICE

If my husband wakes
And finds that I'm not there?

ALEKO

I have.
Where are you going? For both your sakes,
You'd better stay beside this grave.

ZEMFIRA

My love, run, run!

ALEKO

No, stop!

ZEMFIRA

My dear! . . .

ALEKO

Not so fast, my lad! Stay here –

(*Thrusts his knife into him.*)

ZEMFIRA

Aleko!

GYPSY

I am dying!

ZEMFIRA

Aleko!
You'll kill him! Look – you're smeared with blood!
What have you done?

ALEKO

Now taste his love.

ZEMFIRA

I hate you, despise you – I am above
All threats from you: the Devil take you,
You murderer . . .

ALEKO

So, well and good –
You die too!

(*Strikes her.*)

ZEMFIRA

. . . die for my love . . .

Brightly the eastern heavens shone:
Blood-steeped, and with knife in hand,
Out in the steppe beyond the mound
Aleko sat upon the stone,

And there before him on the ground
Two corpses lay; the murderer
Was dreadful to behold. All round
The stricken gypsies were astir.
Off to one side they dug a grave.
The women, each with covered head,
Kissed the eyelids of the dead.
The old man sat alone, his gaze
Firm-fixed upon his daughter's form,
Silent, immobile, and forlorn.
They took the corpses, in the bare
Earth's bosom laid the youthful pair.
Aleko watched them from afar . . .
And when the grave was filled at last
He slowly, as if unaware,
Slipped from the stone, to fall in grass.

Then the old man stood up, came near,
And spoke: "Proud man, be gone from here!
We are untamed, we have no laws –
We do not torture, execute,
We have no need of groans and blood –
But cannot live with murderers . . .
Not for freedom were you born,
You want it for yourself alone;
Your voice is dreadful to our ears:
We are shy and good at heart,

You, bold and evil – so depart,
Farewell to you, may you find peace."

Thus the old man; the wanderer band
Was thereupon in noisy flight
From the disaster of the night.
Soon quite deserted was the land,
But for a solitary cart,
Covered with a wretched hide,
Which rested on the fateful sward.
Thus, out of the late autumn mist
A tardy flock of cranes at dawn
Will rise and call, head south – one, pierced
By lead, will stay behind, forlorn,
Trailing its wounded wing. Night came;
No one lit a cheering flame
Inside the cart; beneath its awning
No one fell asleep till morning.

EPILOGUE

Thus by the magic power of song,
Out of memory's slumbering haze
Visions are brought to life, and throng,
Sometimes of bright, sometimes dark days.

In that far land where war's alarm
For long years never ceased to toll,
Where Russia stretched her mighty arm
To show her frontiers to Stamboul,
And where our double-headed eagle
Still proudly flies without an equal,
There on the steppe I used to meet them,
The gypsies, as their wagons rolled
Across the lines of camps of old,
Children of a humble freedom.
I often roamed the wilderness
Behind their easygoing press,
I shared with them their simple fare
And fell asleep before their fire.
How grateful to my ears on long
Slow journeys was their joyful song,
And to my lips there often came
Sweet Mariyula's gentle name.

But even amongst you innocents
There is no lasting happiness! . . .

Inside your worn and tattered tents
Surge dreams of violence and distress,
And as you wander through the steppe
Catastrophe in hiding waits,
Dark passions everywhere run deep,
There is no refuge from the Fates.

THE BRIDEGROOM

For three whole days the merchant's daughter,
    Natasha, disappeared;
The third night came: in wild disorder
    Natasha reappeared.
Mother and father plied their questions,
Tried to bring about confessions.
    Natasha doesn't hear,
    She scarcely breathes from fear.

Her mother grieved, her father grieved,
    Long did they catechize her,
But when at last she was reprieved
    They still were none the wiser.
Natasha won back cheer and health,
Soon she was her former self
    And with her sisters sat
    Outside the shingle-gate.

There she is with her companions
    Beside the gate one day,
The merchant's girl, when all at once
    A troika gallops by.
Its young and dashing driver tugs
The reins of horses wrapped with rugs;
    He stands up in his sleigh,
    He'll crush all in his way.

He glances at her as he drives,
Natasha glances back,
On like the wind he whirls, he leaves
Natasha thunderstruck.
Back to the house headlong she flies.
"I recognized him – *him!*" she cries –
"I know that it was him!
Stop him, save me from him!"

Shaking their heads, the family gather
And listen full of gloom;
"Daughter dear," begins the father,
"Tell me the truth now, come:
If someone has offended you,
Give us some sign, and that will do."
Natasha doesn't speak.
All she can do is weep.

Next day, betimes, a matchmaker
Is waiting in the parlor.
She utters praises for Natasha,
Then turns toward the father:
"We're buying – you've the goods for us,
And handsome is as handsome does:
The lad has strength and style,
He's free of guile and bile.

"He's wealthy, and he's also clever,
He doesn't touch his cap,
Lives like a boyar, lacked he's never,
Luck drops into his lap;
He'll have a mind to give the girl
A fox-fur coat, a precious pearl,
Gold rings and necklaces,
A rich-brocaded dress.

"He passed your gateway yesterday;
He isn't one that dithers,
So let's to church now – what do you say?
And take the icons with us?"
She sits and eats a plate of pie,
She talks with sighs and slanted eye,
And what the poor bride hears
Rouses her deepest fears.

"It's settled, then," agrees the father,
"Aren't you the lucky one?
My dear Natasha, to the altar!
It's dull to sit alone.
To go through life unwed is wrong,
The linnet has to leave off song,
It's time to build a nest,
Have children and be blessed."

Natasha leans against the wall,
She tries to speak – instead
Begins to sob and shake and wail,
Laugh as though off her head.
The matchmaker, in the disorder,
Runs to her with a flask of water
To offer a drink – then splash a
Dash of it on Natasha.

A family in calamity . . .
Natasha now comes to:
"Your will is sacred, I shall be
Obedient to you.
Call my bridegroom to the feast,
Bake for a hundred guests at least,
Make mead that's good and strong,
And bring the law along."

"We shall now, angel of my heart!
I'd place your happiness
Before my life!" At once they start,
They bake their very best.
And now the worthy guests assemble,
And see, the bride is led to table;
The bridesmaids weep and sing –
A sleigh comes galloping.

The groom! Now everyone is present.
The goblets clash and clink,
The loving cup is found most pleasant;
Guests take their fill of drink.

BRIDEGROOM

"Dear friends, I must be satisfied:
Why does my own and fairest bride
Not drink, nor eat, nor serve?
Why does my fair bride grieve?"

"I'll tell you all I have to tell,"
To the bridegroom spoke the bride.
"My life is now a life in hell,
I weep all day and night.
An evil dream oppresses me."
The father: "What can this dream be?
Dear daughter, if you please,
Put our minds at ease."

"My dream was this," she spoke out loud.
"I wandered in a wood
At night; behind a bank of cloud
A half-moon dimly stood;
I'd lost my path, and all around
No living soul, no living sound,
Nothing at all that stirs,
Only the tops of firs.

"And suddenly, as if I woke,
I saw, close by, a hut.
I knocked – no answer. Then I spoke –
The door stayed firmly shut.
I opened it, prayed, and went inside:
A candle burned, and in its light –
Gold, silver, everywhere . . .
All shining, sumptuous ware."

BRIDEGROOM

"How is your dream an evil one,
Foretelling wealth untold?"

BRIDE

"Wait, sir, till my account is done.
On silver and on gold,
And cloths and carpets and brocade,
And silken stuffs from Novgorod –
On marvels heaven-sent
I gazed in wonderment.

"Then I heard shouts, and clop clop clop . . .
Up to the porch they drove.
I slammed the door – in one quick hop
I hid behind the stove.
Soon I heard voices once again . . .
Into the hut tramped twelve young men,
And with them was a maiden,
A pure and lovely maiden.

"They entered in a noisy horde,
And none took off his hat;
To table, icons quite ignored,
Without a grace they sat,
The eldest brother at their head,
The youngest brother on his right,
And on his left the maiden,
The pure and lovely maiden.

"Laughter and clamor, singing, yelling,
Unbridled merriment . . ."

BRIDEGROOM

"How can your dream be bad, foretelling
Good fortune and content?"

BRIDE

"Wait sir, till my account is done.
The din and revelry went on,
The merriment was mad,
Only the maid was sad.

"She spoke no word, she sat in grief,
Would take no food, no mead.
The eldest brother grasped his knife
And, whistling, whetted it;
He glanced towards the lovely maid,
He gripped her swiftly by the braid,
The villain killed her and
Cut off her right hand."

The bridegroom, with a shrug, replied:
"But this is downright drivel!
You mustn't grieve, beloved bride,
Your dream cannot mean evil."
The bride is swift to answer him:
"Whose hand does it come from, then, this ring?" –
She looks him in the face;
Each guest starts from his place.

The ring rolls clinking on the floor,
The bridegroom has turned pale;
All is confusion. – Speaks the law:
"Bind the criminal!"
Fettered, the villain was condemned
Without delay and met his end.
Natasha's was the glory!
And that is all our story.

COUNT NULIN

Time to be off! Loud blows the horn;
The whippers-in in hunting dress
Have mounted promptly with the dawn,
The close-leashed borzois prance and press.
The master of the house appears,
And pausing in the porch awhile
He looks about; his visage bears
A broad, proprietorial smile.
He wears a girded Cossack coat,
In which a Turkish knife is stowed,
A rum flask hangs below his throat,
A horn upon a bronzen chain.
His blear-eyed wife, in cap and shawl,
Looks from her window, vexed, it's plain,
By all the din and caterwaul . . .
They bring the master of the house
His mount; he grabs the withers, gets
Foot firmly in the stirrup, shouts
Not to wait up – and off he sets.

The period to September's close
(To use the lowly terms of prose)
Can drive the country-dweller mad:
The wind, the sleet, the mud, the haze,
The howl of wolves – but then how glad
The hunter! Scorning easy ways
He thunders through remote terrain,
Spends nights in every kind of place,

Curses, gets soaked and chilled in rain,
Toasts the annihilating chase.

Now what can occupy the spouse
Forsaken by the other spouse?
Not hard to find activities:
She must salt mushrooms, feed the geese,
Make sure the kitchen tasks are heeded,
Inspect the cellar and the barn –
Mistress's eye is always needed
To see that nothing comes to harm.

I'm sad to say, our heroine . . .
(Oh dear! I quite forgot to name her:
"Natasha" she had always been,
But let us properly proclaim her
Natalya Pavlovna) . . . I fear
That our Natalya Pavlovna
Had absolutely no idea
What her domestic duties were;
Her childhood had been spent, alas,
Not under sound paternal rule
But at a gentle boarding school
Run by a Madame Falbalas.

Upon a window seat she sits,
Holding opened on her knees

A sentimental novel; it's
The Love of Armand and Élise:
Or, Two Families' Correspondence,
Volume the Fourth – a classical,
Old-fashioned, long, long, long, long novel,
All moral and respectable,
With none of your Romantic nonsense.

At first Natalya Pavlovna
Had read this epic all agog,
But soon a fight distracted her
Between a yard-goat and a dog.
Boys gathered round with many a hoot.
Meanwhile, a turkey flock pursued
A sodden cockerel, gravely gobbling;
Around a pool three ducks went hobbling,
Then paddled in, and splashed and rolled;
A peasant-woman crossed the mud
To hang a pile of washing out.
It presently grew very cold –
Soon there'd be snow upon the ground . . .
And now there came a coach-bell's sound.

He who has lived the life apart
In rural gloom, my friends, knows well
How strongly it can stir the heart,
That jingle of a distant bell.

A friend come visiting at last,
Some comrade from our dashing past?
It surely can't be *her*? . . . Good lord!
Nearer, nearer . . . The heart beats loud . . .
But further, further fades the sound,
And dies; the listener is ignored.

Natalya Pavlovna with glee
Runs quickly to the balcony:
Over the river, past the mill
A carriage speeds toward her – oh!
Crosses the bridge, draws nearer – no,
Turns left. Near tears, she gazes still.

But – joy! – an unexpected slope –
The carriage topples. "Filka, Vash!
Where are you? Quick, there's been a crash!
Ask them in at once. I hope
The gentleman will dine with me!
Is he alive? Just run and see,
Be quick!"

The servant hurries out.
And now our heroine flies about,
Throws on a shawl, fluffs up her hair,
Adjusts a curtain, moves a chair,
And waits. "Dear God, please bring them here."

At last, at long last, they appear.
Bespattered with the journey's dirt,
Somehow, severely bruised and hurt,
The sorry carriage crawls along.
Behind, a youthful gentleman
Limps. His undaunted serving man,
A Frenchman, cries: "*Courage, allons!*"
They reach the porch, now here they are
Inside the house. Dear reader, while
A bedroom is prepared in style,
Its door is opened wide, Picard
Bustles about and mutters oaths,
His master seeks a change of clothes –
Let me describe the visitor.
Count Nulin, home from foreign tour,
Has squandered his inheritance
In fashionable extravagance.
He's on his way to Petropole,
For show like some rare animal,
With store of hats and fans and waistcoats,
Cufflinks and corsets, cloaks and dress coats,
Pins, studs, and stockings *à la mode*,
Handkerchiefs with colored edges,
Lorgnettes, a book of wicked sketches,
Guizot's new volume (utter rot!),
A novel by Sir Walter Scott –
He has the Paris Court's bons mots,

The latest song by Béranger,
Arias from Rossini, Paër,
And so on and so forth – you know.

The table was laid a while ago;
Impatiently the hostess sighs.
Enter, at last, the visitor.
Up starts Natalya Pavlovna,
Her questions courteously she plies:
His leg now, does it hurt to touch?
Oh, says the count, it's nothing much.
To table then without ado.
The count moves his place nearer hers,
And starts the conversation: first
He curses Holy Russia – who
Can live in such perpetual snow?
He misses life in Paris so . . .
"How is the theatre?" "In decline,
C'est bien mauvais, ça fait pitié:
Talma's quite deaf, his voice – a whine,
And Mamselle Mars shows every sign . . .
But then Potier, *le grand Potier!*
He is the most admired by far,
As much as he has ever been."
"Which writers are most popular?"
"Oh, d'Arlincourt and Lamartine."
"In Russia they're much imitated."

"Is that so? Then the Russian mind
 Is really not so far behind?
 God grant we'll soon be educated!"
"Where is the waist-line?" "Very low –
 Almost to . . . This is now the line.
 But your *toilette* – it's very fine:
 Those ruches, bows, and that design . . .
 All very much the mode, you know."
"We take the *Moscow Telegraph*."
"Oh, really? . . . Would you care for some
 Vaudeville? This will make you laugh."
 The count proceeds to sing. "Count, come,
 Please help yourself." "No more, I can't."

They rise. The hostess is in bliss.
Paris forgotten now, the count
Marvels at her: how sweet she is!
The evening passes quickly by;
The count is quite beside himself;
His hostess's expressive eye
Now warms, now sinks in mute reply . . .
And all too soon the clock strikes twelve.
His man snores in the portico,
The neighbor's cockerel starts to crow,
The watchman strikes his iron bar,
All candles in the room are spent.
Rising, Natalya Pavlovna
Declares the evening at an end,

Wishes the count a good night's rest.
The dizzy, disappointed guest
Kisses her hand . . . And now, guess what!
What end to coquetry? The tease –
And may she be forgiven by God –
Gives the count's hand a gentle squeeze.

Natalya Pavlovna undresses;
Parasha stands behind her chair.
To this Parasha she confesses
Her every daily thought and care:
Parasha washes, sews, brings news,
Is grateful for cast-off fichus,
Provokes her master into laughter
And rails at him the moment after,
Lies to her mistress brazenly.
Now she holds forth imposingly
About the count and his affairs;
The thorough knowledge that she airs!
Heaven knows where she has it from.
At last her mistress, with a frown –
"That's enough of your going on!" –
Demands her nightclothes, then lies down
And tells Parasha to be gone.

Meanwhile the count retires to rest;
Helped by his man, he gets undressed . . .
Climbs into bed. Monsieur Picard

Offers his master a cigar,
A silver tumbler and a bottle,
Lamp, tweezers, clock, and uncut novel.

In bed, our hero runs his eyes
Over a page of Walter Scott.
He grasps, however, not a jot,
Distracted by a wild surmise . . .
"Could I," he wonders, "Heavens above!
Could I really be in love?
How entertaining that would be,
What an adventure, what delight!
My hostess likes the look of me . . ."
Nulin extinguishes the light.

But sleep just will not come to him;
A fever runs through every limb.
The Devil fills his wakeful mind
With fancies of a sinful kind.
Our ardent hero with a sigh
Imagines that vivacious eye,
That rather full and rounded figure,
That voice's pleasing female flow,
That face's rosy country glow –
Finer than paint are health and vigor.
And oh! that shapely little foot,
And oh! the simple way she put
Her hand in his, and lightly squeezed!

The moment ought to have been seized –
How foolish to have left her. But
Time yet. Her door will not be shut . . .
Donning his striped silk dressing gown,
The count is speedily abroad.
In the dark a chair goes down;
Tarquin, in hope of sweet reward,
Once more sets forth to seek Lucretia,
Resolved to go through fire to reach her.

Thus you may see a cunning tom,
The mincing darling of the house,
Slip from the stove to stalk a mouse,
Creep stealthily and slowly on
Towards his victim, grow slit-eyed
And wave his tail from side to side,
Coil to a ball, extend his claws
And snap! the wretch is in his paws.

On through the darkness groped the count
With passion burning in his breast,
Scarcely daring to draw breath
And trembling at each sudden sound
The floorboards gave. At last he found
The sanctum door; a gentle press
Upon the stout brass handle – yes!
Slowly, softly the door uncloses . . .
Inside the bedroom, fitfully

A lamp still burns, and palely glows as
The mistress peacefully reposes,
Asleep, or she pretends to be.

He enters, half-withdraws, and sighs –
Falls at her feet at last . . . I urge
You ladies of St. Petersburg:
Picture the wild awakening eyes
Of my Natalya Pavlovna –
What shall she do? Decide for her.

She stared in sheer bewilderment;
Our hero showered her with grand,
If imitative, sentiment,
And coolly his audacious hand
Reached out to touch her eiderdown.
At first she was too numbed to frown . . .
Then realization dawned upon her,
And full of fury for her honor,
Also, we may suppose, of fear,
With sure and swiftly swinging hand
She didn't hesitate to land
A good hard blow on Tarquin's ear!

Count Nulin burned with deepest shame
At such an insult to his name.
I wonder how things might have gone,
That cut to self-esteem so deep,

Had not the barking of the pom
Woken Parasha from her sleep.
He heard her footsteps drawing close,
He cursed his refuge of the night,
The willful beauty, and he rose
To take shamefaced and rapid flight.

How the assorted company
Spent the remainder of the night –
I'll leave imaginations free,
I don't intend to say who's right.

Comes morning. Taciturn, our guest
Rises and lazily gets dressed;
Carelessly, yawning, trims his nails,
Clumsily ties his kerchief, fails
To smooth moist locks. A call to tea
Breaks in upon his reverie.
What should he do? He strives to bury
His painful shame and secret fury,
And leaves the room.

His hostess dips
Her mischievous and mocking eyes
And, biting pretty scarlet lips,
In various wary ways she tries
A conversation. Shy and cold
At first, our hero grows more bold,

And gives his answers with a smile.
He banters with a pleasant art;
Within a very little while
He has once more half-lost his heart.
There comes a clamor from the hall.
Who's there? "Natasha!"
"Heavens above!...
Here is my husband, count. – My love,
Count Nulin."
"Glad to have you call...
What nasty weather, my, it's raw...
I passed the forge just now and saw
Your carriage – it's in good repair.
Natasha dear! We caught a hare
Outside the orchard... Vodka now!
It's not from these parts, count, you know –
I'll fetch you some, if you'll allow...
You'll lunch with us before you go?"
"Well, I don't know, I shouldn't stay."
"No, count, you mustn't be away,
My wife and I are glad of guests.
Do stay!"
But still the count requests
They let him leave. His hopes are gone,
He is both furious and forlorn.
Picard, well strengthened by a glass,
Grunts with a heavy traveling case.
Two servants hurry out to lash

The trunk upon the equipage
Which now draws up outside the door.
Picard has seen to everything;
The count departs at last. What more
Can I relate? A word, my friends,
To add before my story ends.

Away our hero's carriage rolled.
Natalya Pavlovna soon told
Her husband, neighbors, everyone
Just how my count had made so bold.
And who laughed more than anyone
To hear Natalya Pavlovna?
You'll never guess. – Whyever not?
Her husband! – No sir. Of the lot,
He was the least amused by far;
He called the count a fool, a whelp,
He'd vouch for it, he'd make him yelp,
He'd raise his pack of hounds to help.
No, Lidin laughed most heartily,
Their neighbor (who was twenty-three).

I think we may now truly say
Fidelity need not give rise –
Not even, my dear friends, today –
To any very great surprise.

THE TALE OF THE DEAD PRINCESS AND THE SEVEN CHAMPIONS

A king went on a journey,
He bade his queen farewell;
She waited by the window
To watch for his return.
She waited and she waited
And watched the empty plain,
Watched from dawn to nightfall;
Her eyes began to burn.
No sign of her dear husband!
All she saw was snow,
The whirling of the blizzard,
White over all the world.
Nine months went by; her vigil
She constantly maintained.
Then on the night of Christmas,
God gave the queen a girl.
Early in the morning
At last the king and sire,
Each day and night expected,
Returned to see his bride.
Setting eyes upon him,
She sighed the deepest sigh,
She could not bear such rapture;
Toward morning mass she died.

Long grieved the king, a twelvemonth
Passed like an empty dream;

But he was only human,
And so once more he wed.
It must be said, the maiden
Was every inch a queen,
Tall and fair and graceful;
She also had a head,
Though prone to obstinacy,
And pride, and jealousy.
Now in the young queen's dowry
There was a looking-glass
With one especial virtue:
The power of human speech.
Only before this mirror
Could she be at ease;
She'd preen herself and banter,
The mirror she'd beseech:
"Mirror, mirror, tell me,
And mind that you speak true:
Am I not the fairest,
Rosiest of all?"
And she would hear the answer:
"No doubt of it, O Queen,
Indeed you are the fairest,
Rosiest of all."
The queen would give a chuckle,
Artfully raise her shoulders,
Throw a glance slit-eyed,

Swiftly snap her fingers,
Turn with arms akimbo,
And view herself with pride.

Meanwhile, the king's young daughter
Quietly grew, and bloomed
A fair-skinned, black-browed beauty,
A kind and gentle soul.
A suitor came to see her,
The young Prince Yelisey.
The king gave his agreement;
Her dowry was in whole
A hundred and forty towers
And seven market towns.

The day before the marriage,
Before the bridal ball,
The queen was at her mirror
And spoke to it once more:
"Am I not still the fairest,
Rosiest of all?"
"Indeed," the mirror answered,
"Fair you are, O Queen;
The princess, though, is fairest,
Rosiest of all."
Up leapt the queen in thunder,
How she raged, and stamped

Upon the looking-glass!
"Ah, you wicked mirror!
You're lying out of spite.
My rival – that jackass!
Just look what she's grown into!
No wonder she's so pale:
Her mother, when she carried her,
Sat staring at the snow!
How can *she*, I ask you,
Be compared with me?
Find me in all our kingdom –
The world! – my equal; no,
Of course I am the fairest."
The mirror on the wall:
"The princess is the fairest,
Rosiest of all."
The queen, with blackest hatred,
Flung the glass to the floor;
Her servant-girl, Chernavka,
She ordered to contrive
A long walk with the princess
Into the deepest forest,
Then bind her up and leave her
For wolves to eat alive.

The Devil cannot answer
A woman in a rage.

Chernavka led the princess
To thickets so far off
She guessed the worst intentions.
Seized by mortal fear,
"Upon my life," she pleaded,
"What am I guilty of?
If you do not kill me,
One day, when I am queen,
Be sure I shall reward you."
The girl was fond of her;
She didn't kill or bind her,
But bade her not be sad,
And saying, "God be with you,"
She now abandoned her . . .
"Where is our young beauty?"
The queen desired to know.
"I left her in the forest,"
She heard the maid's reply,
"Bound firmly by the elbows,
She'll not survive for long;
Should some wild beast get at her,
She'll very quickly die."

Soon all the people knew it:
The young princess was lost!
While the poor king was grieving,
The brave Prince Yelisey,

With many a fervent prayer,
In search of his princess,
In search of his young beauty,
Set forth upon his way.

And through the deepest forest
His young bride walked till dawn;
On and on she wandered,
And came upon a tower.
A dog ran towards her, barking,
And then fell quiet and played.
In she went through the gateway;
Silent was the hour.
Cautiously the princess,
Nuzzled by the dog,
Climbed the steps to the threshold
And grasped the great door-ring:
The door swung gently open
Upon a bright-lit room –
Benches she saw before her
With homely covering,
Icons, an oaken table,
A tiled shelf on the stove.
The princess saw a household
Good-hearted people keep;
She'd surely not be harmed here –
But not a soul in sight.

About the house she hastened,
Ventured to clean and sweep,
Lit a holy candle,
Made sure the stove was hot;
Then she climbed to a plank-bed
And soon was fast asleep.

Now it was time for supper;
Tramping feet in the yard:
In came seven champions,
Red moustaches seven.
The eldest spoke: "A wonder!
Everything bright and clean,
Everything tidy. Someone
Seems to expect us seven.
Who is it? Show yourself,
And be our true companion.
If you are old, you'll be
Our uncle; young, our brother;
If an old woman, you'll be
Our dear and precious mother;
If, though, you're a fair maid –
Sister you'll be, none other."

Now the princess appeared,
And did her seven hosts reverence,
Bowed to the waist and blushed,

And asked for their forgiveness
That she was in their house
But hadn't been invited.
They realized from her speech
That they were hosts to a princess;
They sat her in the ingle,
Before her set a pie
And a glass upon a salver.
But wine she would have none,
And of the pie she tasted
A single piece of crust;
Rest was what she wanted,
Now her day was done.
The brothers led the maiden
Up to a bright-lit room,
Wished her goodnight and left her
Until next day, alone.

The days passed by, the princess
Lived quietly in the wood,
And of the seven champions
Never did she tire.
Before first light the seven
Went forth in happy throng
To try their skill and sinews;
At the gray duck they'd fire,
Or chase the mountain Cherkess

Straying through the wood,
Or down a mounted Saracen,
Or chop a Tatar's pate.
And for her part the princess
Kept house; she cleaned and cooked;
With no dispute or quarrel
Days passed at rapid rate.

To that good maid the brothers
All lost their hearts as one.
They came at break of day
To speak to her, all seven.
The eldest: "Our dear maiden,
Dear sister to us all,
We are in love with you,
Each brother of us seven
Would take you for his own:
But such is not God's ruling;
And so, for mercy's sake,
Let it be decided:
Be wife to one of us
And to the rest, a sister.
Why do you shake your head?
A jewel can't be divided?"

"Oh, faithful, honest brothers,
Brothers most dear to me,"

The princess gave her answer,
"If I deceive you, pray
Almighty God I perish.
I am betrothed. To me,
You're all so wise, so fearless,
I love you equally,
I could not choose between you;
But I have given my heart,
I've made my choice for ever:
It is Prince Yelisey."

The brothers kept their silence,
And stood and scratched their heads.
The eldest of them answered:
"Forgive us," and bowed low;
"If that's the case, you'll never
Hear more from us." "I'm not,"
Replied the princess, "angry,
"I'm only saying no;
It's not your fault." Politely
The suitors left the room;
And so their lives continued
Without dissent or woe.

Meanwhile, the evil stepmother,
Remembering the princess,
Sulked and could not forgive her;

The mirror roused her bile.
At last she went to see it,
Forgot her rage, sat down,
Began to preen before it,
And spoke to it with a smile:
"Mirror, mirror, tell me,
And mind you tell me true:
Now am I not the fairest,
Rosiest on earth?"
"Indeed," the mirror answered,
"Fair you are, O Queen,
But somewhere in the greenwood
A maiden keeps her hearth,
Quietly, with seven champions;
She is most fair on earth."
The queen flew at Chernavka:
"Up to your tricks again!
How could you dare deceive me!"
And brought her to confess.
With an iron penal collar
The cruel queen threatened her,
Vowed one of them must perish –
She or the princess.

One day, beside her window
The princess sat and spun,
Waiting for the champions.

She heard, close by the wall,
The house dog fiercely barking;
She raised her eyes and saw
A holy beggar-woman
Fend off the animal.
"Old woman, wait!" – she started –
"I'll chase the dog away
And bring you down a morsel."
The holy woman: "Child!
That cursed dog half-killed me,
That savage beast of yours –
Come down here and help me!
I've never seen so wild!"
The princess fetched her something,
She'd hardly left the stair –
The dog came swiftly at her,
Barking as if to keep
Its mistress from the stranger;
Fierce as a forest bear
Leapt at the holy woman.
"How strange! He's missed his sleep,"
The princess said; "Catch this now!"
A loaf flew through the air;
The little old woman caught it –
"Thank you kindly," she cried,
"God bless you for your kindness;
And this for you now – catch!"

A fresh and juicy pippin,
A golden one, she shied
To the princess on the stairway . . .
How the dog leapt and whined . . .
But, hands outstretched, the princess
Caught it neat and clean.
"When you're bored, my darling,
Just eat that fruit, and say
Your grace . . ." The little old woman
Bowed, and was no more seen . . .
Up the stairs with the princess,
Looking in her face,
The dog ran, whined its heart out,
And growled, as if to say:
"You mustn't touch that apple!"
The princess smiled at him,
Stroked him, and asked him gently:
"What's up with you today?" –
Then went into her chamber
And quietly shut the door,
To spin before the window
And see the brothers in,
Always eyeing the apple
So ripe and rich with juice,
So pure and fresh and fragrant,
With such a golden skin
It seemed to ooze with honey!

Inside it showed the pips . . .
She tried to wait till supper,
But she could wait no more;
She raised the golden apple
Up to her scarlet lips,
And took a tiny nibble . . .
A piece went down her throat . . .
And now the poor thing, breathless,
Shakes to her fingertips,
Her pure white hands fall lifeless
And drop the golden fruit,
She falls beneath the icons
And upward roll her eyes;
Her head upon a wall-bench,
Motionless she lies . . .

And now the seven brothers
Returned in merry throng,
Fresh from some bold adventure.
Towards them, head lifted high,
The dog came howling, led them
Home to the tower. "For sure,"
The brothers cried, "misfortune
Awaits us here!" Inside
They sped – O woe! Next moment
The dog rushed in and snatched
The apple, barking, snarling –

Gulped it down. And more
He never breathed: that apple
Was poisoned to the core.
Before the lifeless princess
The seven in their grief
Spoke a holy prayer,
And stood with heads bowed deep.
They raised her up and dressed her
For burial – but paused,
In doubt if they should do so.
As on the breast of sleep
She lay, so fresh and peaceful
It seemed as if she breathed.
Three days the brothers waited;
The princess did not wake.
Done with the doleful ritual,
The body of the maid
They laid in a crystal coffin,
And then set forth to take
Her corpse at hour of midnight
To a far-off mountain cave;
There they affixed the coffin
To six stout pillars, girt
With six stout chains of iron,
And round it built a grille.
And there they paid their sister
Their last respects on earth:

"Sleep in your grave," – the eldest –
"On earth your beauty fell
All too soon to evil;
Heaven receive your soul.
With all our hearts we loved you,
And kept you for your love –
But you belonged to no man,
Now the grave has you whole."

The wicked queen, that morning,
Eager to hear good news,
Went to take her mirror
In secret from the wall.
"Am I not the fairest,
Rosiest of all?"
Asked she, and came the answer:
"No doubt of it, O Queen,
Indeed you are the fairest,
Rosiest of all."

Meanwhile, ever seeking
His dear-beloved bride,
Round the world and weeping
Rode Prince Yelisey.
But always those he questioned
Were hard put for reply;
They answered him with laughter

Or simply turned away.
At last he put his question
To the glorious golden Sun:
"Dear Sun! All year you wander
About the skies, you bring
Warm spring to end the winter,
You see all humankind.
You'll not refuse to help me? –
Have you, while journeying,
Seen a fair young princess?
I'm her betrothed." "Dear friend,"
The golden Sun gave answer,
"A princess? No. I fear
She'll be no longer living;
Although, perhaps, the Moon,
My neighbor, may have met her,
Or seen some sign of her."

And so the Prince, in torment,
Waited for the night.
And when the Moon had risen,
He promptly put his case:
"O Moon, my dear companion,
Heavenly silver horn!
You get up in the darkness,
Bright-eyed and round of face;
All the stars admire you,

They love to see you rise.
You'll not refuse to help me? –
Have you, wherever you've been,
Seen a fair young princess?
I'm her betrothed." "My friend,"
The brilliant Moon gave answer,
"No princess have I seen.
But I am only watchman
When it is my turn,
I might have missed the princess."
The king's son in reply:
"My bride is lost forever!"
The Moon: "No, wait; perhaps
The Wind has seen her. Ask him.
Do not be sad – goodbye."

Prince Yelisey, now heartened,
Sped on to ask the Wind:
"Wind, you are strong and mighty,
You chase the cloudy flocks,
And stir the dark blue ocean,
And blow through all the world,
You fear no higher power,
You only bow to God's.
You'll not refuse to help me? –
Have you, while blustering,
Seen a fair young princess?

I'm her betrothed." "Well now,"
The wild Wind spoke in answer,
"I know a quiet stream,
A craggy peak beyond it,
With a cavern deep below,
And in that dismal cavern
A crystal coffin hangs
On chains from six stout pillars.
There, in that mountainside
Which carries no man's footprint,
You will find your bride."

Onward the wild Wind hastened.
Sobbing bitterly,
Prince Yelisey pressed forward
To that deserted place
To see his heart's beloved
One last time. He saw
The barren land before him;
To that steep mountain face,
To that deep cavern's entrance
He swiftly made his way.
There in dismal darkness
A crystal coffin hangs,
And in that crystal coffin
The princess lies at peace.
Upon his dear bride's coffin

In grief he beats and bangs.
The coffin cracks. The maid
Immediately awakens.
Amazed, she looks about:
"How long I have been sleeping!"
She sighs a mighty sigh,
And from the hanging coffin
Out with care she climbs . . .
Ah! The pair are weeping.
By the hand he takes her
And leads her to the light;
Happily conversing,
Homeward they make their way;
"Our young princess is living!"
The trumpeters convey.

Now the evil stepmother
Idly sat at home,
Talking to the mirror
That hung upon the wall:
"Am I not the fairest,
Rosiest of all?"
And this she heard for answer:
"Yes, fair you are, O Queen,
The princess, though, is fairest,
Rosiest of all."
Up leapt the wicked stepmother,

She smashed the glass to bits,
Rushed straight out through the doorway,
And met the young princess.
A pang went through and through her,
She died of her distress.
The moment she was buried
The marriage was prepared,
And with his heart's intended
Prince Yelisey was wed.
There followed celebration
Unknown before to man;
I was among the guests there –
My whiskers scarcely wet.

THE TALE OF THE GOLDEN COCKEREL

Somewhere in the Thrice-Ninth Clime,
In the Thrice-Eleventh Time,
Reigned the glorious Tsar Dadon.
Formidable from boyhood on,
He would unrelentingly
Cause offense and injury;
When, however, he grew old,
His campaigns were not so bold,
He desired a rest from war.
Then his neighbors by the score
Shook the tsar from his repose,
Dealt him many fearful blows.
Every outpost sent alarms;
Men in thousands under arms
He was driven to maintain,
Guarding his besieged terrain.
Generals did what they could do;
Hopeless, they were far too few:
Danger from the south they guessed –
In came raiders from the west;
Mended one catastrophe –
Evil visitors by sea.
Tears of rage shed Tsar Dadon,
Sleepless nights had turned him wan.
What a life, in such despair!
Seeking counsel everywhere,
One astrologer the monarch

Chose from his wise men, a eunuch;
Sent for him by courier.

And without delay the seer
Came before Dadon; he took
From his bag a golden cock.
Thus he spoke before his sire:
"Set this cockerel on a spire;
He will keep good watch for you,
This my golden bird and true:
When he sees it's quiet all round
He will sit without a sound;
But should ever foe be spied
Creeping up on any side,
Some approaching armored horde,
Something, somewhere, untoward –
Then my golden bird will rise,
Raise his comb toward the skies,
Ruffle up his plumes and crow;
He will turn toward the foe."
Tsar Dadon, at last consoled,
Promised quantities of gold.
"For the service you have done,"
To the eunuch glad Dadon,
"Whatsoever is your will
As my own I shall fulfill."

So the cock with faithful eye
Watched the frontiers from on high.
Danger spied, he'd stir and shuffle,
Face the foe with plumes a-ruffle:
"Now Tsar – cock-a doodle-do! –
What an easy life for you!"
And the neighbors of Dadon,
Soundly beaten one by one,
Once more held the tsar in awe:
By and by they ceased to war.

Two years passed; without a sound
Sat the cockerel; calm all round.
Then one day a mighty rumpus
Roused the ruler from his slumbers.
"Father of the people! Save us!"
At his door a general quavers,
"Sire, awake! Calamity!"
"What d'you want, good man, of me?
What calamity?" Dadon
Answers slowly with a yawn.
"Listen, sire – the cock is crowing:
In the city, fear is growing."
To the window! Facing west,
See! the cockerel crows its best.
"Warriors – no time to waste!
Every man to horse! Make haste!"

Off behind his elder son
Sets the army of Dadon.
Now the cock turns from the west,
Peace; the tsar returns to rest.

Seven days and not a word
From his army to be heard;
Was there, was there not, a battle?
No word reached the capital.
Once again the cockerel crows.
Off a second army goes;
Now his younger son Dadon
Sends to save the elder one.
Soon the cockerel crows no more.
No word back, just as before!
Seven days again go past,
All the city is aghast;
Once again the cockerel crows;
Off Dadon's third army goes:
Whether or no it's for the best,
This one he leads toward the west.

Night and day his men of war
Marched till they could march no more:
Not a sign of battle found,
Bivouac or burial mound.
Tsar Dadon, in puzzlement

As to what this mystery meant,
Led his men through passes high;
Seven days again go by,
And upon the mountainside,
See! a silken tent is spied.
All is silent, all serene;
Close by, down a deep ravine
Lie the armies he has sent.
Tsar Dadon draws near the tent . . .
Horror! Both his sons lie dead,
Armorless, with naked head,
Plunged in each the other's sword;
Back and forth upon the sward,
On the trampled bloody grass,
Their abandoned horses pass . . .
Cried the tsar: "My sons – my sons!
Our two falcons both at once
Fallen to the snare! Oh woe!
Now my hour has come, I know."
All lamented with Dadon,
Valleys groaned with grievous groan,
And the mountain's heart was rent.
Suddenly the silken tent
Opened wide its flaps, and ah! –
Slowly, softly toward the tsar
Walked a maiden like the dawn,
Walked the Queen of Shamakhan.

As in sun the bird of shade,
He was mute before the maid,
Gazing long upon her eyes
He forgot his sons' demise.
She with bow and smiling face
Led him to her dwelling place,
Seated him before her table,
There to feast all he was able;
Then she bade him lay his head
On a rich-brocaded bed.
Seven days passed by again;
Willing slave in her domain,
With the maiden queen Dadon,
Charmed, enraptured, feasted on.

Then the tsar, so long delayed,
With his warriors and the maid
Set off on his journey home
By the route that he had come.
All the way before him flew
Rumor true and not so true.
From the town gates with a shout
All the people hastened out,
Hailed the chariot from afar –
Ran behind the queen and tsar;
All were greeted by Dadon . . .
Now he sees amidst the throng,

White in sage's hat and tunic,
All swan-white, his friend the eunuch.
"Father! What have you to say?
Closer . . . Your petition, pray?"
Thus the wise man: "Let us clear,
Now at last, accounts, O Tsar.
Long ago you promised me,
For my services in fee
Whatsoever was my will
As your own you would fulfill.
Give me therefore, sire, the Queen,
Give me the Shamàkhan Queen."
Answered Tsar Dadon in thunder:
"What is this I hear? – I wonder,
Has the Devil seized your wits?
So, I promised . . . It befits
Age and wisdom to maintain
Limits! You – to play the swain?
Don't you know, then, who I am?
Ask for gold, a boyar's name,
Horses from the royal stud,
Half my kingdom if you would!"
"I'll have none of these – the Queen,
Give me the Shamàkhan Queen,"
Said the wise man to the tsar.
"Devil take you! You, I swear,"
Spat the tsar, "will never win her.

You torment yourself, you sinner –
Off, while you possess your soul!
Take away this doddering fool!"
Still the old man would persist;
Best not though, with some, insist:
Now his brow the scepter found,
Laid him out upon the ground
Stone dead. – All the city shuddered . . .
No lament the maiden uttered:
"Ha-ha-ha!" and "He-he-he!" –
Unafraid of sin was she.
Tsar Dadon, alarmed the while,
Turned on her a tender smile.
On he drove toward the town . . .
Came a gentle ringing: down –
Full in view of all the people –
Flew the cockerel from its steeple;
Met the chariot as it sped,
Perched upon the tsar's bare head,
Plumes a-ruffle, pecked his pate,
Up and off . . . From lofty state
On the instant Tsar Dadon
Fell – and perished with a groan.
Wholly vanished was the queen,
Quite as if she'd never been.
This my tale, though not the truth,
Holds a lesson for our youth.

NOTES

In these notes transliteration from the Cyrillic alphabet is intended to approximate actual sounds. Spoken Russian stress (as opposed to metrical stress, which is often notional) is marked.

Original texts followed are those of the Complete Edition of Pushkin published by the Soviet Academy of Sciences (Moscow and Leningrad, 1937–59), reprinted by Voskresenye (Moscow, 1994–97), vol. 2, part 1; vol. 3, part 1; vols. 4–5.

The Gypsies

Page 3, line 1: *Bessarabia.* Successively colonized by the Greeks, Romans, Genoese, and Ottomans, this territory bordering the northwest of the Black Sea – today divided between Moldova, Ukraine, and Romania – was ceded to Russia in 1812 on the conclusion of the fourth of the many Russo-Turkish wars.

Page 4, line 14: *a mound. Kurgàny* (singular: *kurgàn*), ancient burial mounds, are found in large number in the southern Russian steppes. They have, of course, nothing to do with the humbler and more modern graves that also feature in the poem.

Page 4, line 19: *Aleko is his name.* Also a form of Pushkin's. Pronounced *Alyèko.*

Page 5, line 13: *couch of bliss.* Pushkin's diction here, *lòzhe nyègi,* as also occasionally elsewhere in the poem, was thought too archaically poetic by some contemporaries.

Page 6, lines 15–17: *doleful ... abandoned ... melancholy ...* A change of stylistic register to the Byronic-Romantic after the sharply observed realism of the opening passages. This mode continues until it modulates into the more focused style of the Old Man relating the legend of Ovid's southern exile; it is resumed in Aleko's utterances (asleep and awake) and actions following the section containing Zemfira's song.

Page 7, lines 1–16: *God's little bird knows neither ... Beyond the dark blue sea.* In these sixteen lines Pushkin changes the meter to trochaic tetrameter, his favorite "folk" meter, which he uses in *The Dead Princess* and *The Golden Cockerel.* I have rendered the contrast in a trimeter mixing iambic and trochaic lines.

The folk motif of the "little bird beyond the sea" in the last line comes again in the lyric "Winter Evening," written a few months later during Pushkin's exile at Mikhaylovskoye.

Page 8, line 15–page 11, line 20: *Zemfira: Tell me, my love ... A smoke-filled tent for all his stage?* Pushkin added this fourth section after he had made a fair copy of what had at first been the whole poem including the epilogue. Later still he added eight autobiographical lines to the epilogue (see the second note to page 30).

Page 10, lines 5–8: *It's said that once an emperor / Banished a subject ... his strange name).* The Emperor Augustus banished Ovid in A.D. 8 to Tomis on the western shore of the Black Sea, to the south of Bessarabia – present-day Constanţa in Romania – apparently because of an unfortunate coincidence between *The Art of Love* and adultery scandals in the imperial family. Ovid spent the last ten years of his life in Tomis. The Old Man's account of Ovid's exile chimes with the poet's own in *Tristia*, which Pushkin had read in French translation three years earlier in Kishinev, Bessarabia, occasioning the poem "To Ovid," which he wrote at that time.

Page 14, line 1: *The old man warms in springtime sun.* Having completed the poem, Pushkin drafted a passage including a thirty-nine-line diatribe against the "depravity of civilization" addressed by Aleko to his newborn son, to precede this line, but abandoned it.

Page 14, line 5: *Old husband, dread husband* . . . The words and rhythm of Zemfira's song are based on a Moldavian folk song. Pushkin's words, along with much else from *The Gypsies*, feature in Bizet's *Carmen* (see Introduction, page XXVI).

Page 20, line 14: *Mòskaly.* Pushkin uses the contemptuous Slavic, especially Polish, term *Moskàl* for "Muscovite."

Page 20, lines 17, 18: *Akkerman.* Turkish fortress on the mouth of the Dniester; it became Russian at the beginning of the war with Turkey of 1806–12. *The Budzhak plain.* In southern Bessarabia.

Page 21, line 5: *Maryula.* Pushkin consistently has "Mariyula" (four syllables), but I have spelled and stressed three ways to suit the meter, and as one varies the form of a loved person's name.

Page 21, line 6: *The Kagul.* A tributary of the Danube; a Russian victory on this river in 1770 paved the way for Russian entry to the Danube.

Page 27, lines 3, 6: *I hate you, despise you . . . die for my love.* Here Pushkin has verbal echoes of Zemfira's song; I have made the echoes metrical as well, with iambic breaking into anapestic. "I die loving" (*Umiràyu lyubyà*) is a stock-in-trade of early Russian Romantic verse, and concludes Pushkin's poem "Desire," written when he was seventeen.

Page 28, line 18: *Proud man.* Pushkin first wrote "violent man" (*bùynyy chelovyèk*). His amendment gets to the heart of the difference between Aleko and the gypsies.

Page 28, lines 19–22: *We are untamed ... But cannot live with murderers ...* The Old Man's argument has its own logic: gypsies have no laws, and so do not exact punishment; yet, wild and lawless though they are, they cannot accept murder or associate with murderers: it is law-based "civilization" that produces violence.

Page 29, line 14: *Trailing its wounded wing.* One of Pushkin's sketches of gypsy tents in his working notebook is rather suggestive of the shape of a trailing wing.

Page 30, lines 5–6: *where war's alarm / For long years never ceased to toll.* See the first note to this poem.

Page 30, lines 15–22: *I often roamed ... Sweet Mariyula's gentle name.* Pushkin added these eight lines some time after he had completed his fair copy.

Page 31, line 1: *worn and tattered tents.* Pushkin repeats his adjective *iz(ò)drannyy*, "tattered" (which I have expanded), from the opening of the poem, as he does the further words for "noisy throng" in the first line of the poem's last paragraph, preceding the epilogue (scattered over two lines in my translation).

Page 31, last line: *the Fates.* Pushkin's friend Vyazemsky found this note of Greek tragedy too heavy an ending to the poem.

The Bridegroom

Page 35, stanza 1: *Natasha, disappeared / ... Natasha reappeared.* Pushkin does not have this repetition, though he does repeat Natasha's name in lines 6 and 7 of this opening stanza. I have taken his overall use of repetition in this ballad as license for it.

Page 36, stanza 1: In Pushkin's dynamic first four lines the ratio of verbs to other parts of speech is almost 1:1, as compared with 1:3 in my translation. In the last three lines my five *him*s keep rough parity with Pushkin's four.

Page 36, stanza 3: The last two lines show Pushkin's concentration: three out of four of his substantive words are rhymed, compared with three out of six in my translation.

Page 37, stanza 3: *linnet* in line 6 suits my translation as Pushkin's "swallow" (*kosàtke*) does his meter.

Page 39, stanza 3: Pushkin's onomatopoeia in the last four lines is unmatchable in translation. No fewer than six *s* and six *sh* sounds create the soughing of a dense wood: *S trapìnki sbìlas' ya: v glushì / Nye slỳshno bylo ni dushì, / I sòsny lish' da yèli / Vershìnami shumyèli.*

Page 40, stanza 3: *clop clop clop*. In a note to *Eugene Onegin*, Pushkin defends his use of words like *top* (the sound of horses' hooves) against reviewers' objections, citing their use in Russian folk literature. "These words are fundamentally Russian," he writes. "One should not interfere with the freedom of our rich and beautiful language."

The final couplet of this stanza is substantially repeated in the next stanza, with the rhyme-words *golubìtsa* ("pure creature") and *devìtsa* ("maiden"), the last line consisting of the weighty double noun *Krasàvitsa-devìtsa* ("Beauty-maiden" or "Maiden-beauty").

Page 41 stanza 3: In the final couplet, consecutive *a*, *u*, and *r* sounds create a savage and sinister expression of the knifer's relish: *Zladèy devìtsu gùbit, / Yey pràvu rùku rùbit.* The exact phrase *pravu ruku* ("right hand") has already been heard in a subliminal pre-echo two stanzas previously; it has had to be lost in my translation "on his right."

Count Nulin

Page 47, lines 7–8: *his visage bears . . . proprietorial smile.* Pushkin's vowels are graphic: *Yegò davòl'noye litsò / Priyàtnoy vàzhnost'yu siyàyet.* Literally: "His satisfied face / With pleasant importance shines." See also the third note to page 93 of *The Tale of the Golden Cockerel.*

Page 47, lines 20–21: *The period . . . prose.* The prosaic elements in *Count Nulin* (including everything about the heroine) irritated reviewers.

Page 48, line 2: *Toasts the annihilating chase.* Pushkin exploits the long polysyllabic Russian adjective: his "toasts" comes at the end of the preceding line, leaving "annihilating chase" to occupy a whole line: *Apustashìtel'nyy nabyèg.*

Page 48, lines 13, 15: *"Natasha" . . . Natalya.* Play with nomenclature. "Natasha" is the name of wholesome "Russian" characters in Pushkin's earlier poems, as in *The Bridegroom*; later "Natalya" comes into its own, with more exalted associations, culminating in the "Madonna," Pushkin's wife. Here the more formal form is a veneer that goes with Natasha's "Europeanism," covering her true rural Russian self. For this analysis I am indebted to an essay by Boris Gasparov; see Introduction, note to page XXXI.

Page 49, line 5: *long, long, long, long novel.* Pushkin's line, reiterating his (longer) adjective three times, is: *Atmyènna dlìnnyy, dlìnnyy, dlìnnyy* ("very long, long, long").

Page 52, line 7: *"Courage, allons!"* Nearly a dozen French phrases and names occur in *Count Nulin* in the Latin alphabet.

Page 52, lines 20 ff: *With store of hats . . . Handkerchiefs . . .* These details are reminiscent of the "young philosopher's" items of toiletry and dress listed in the first chapter of *Eugene Onegin*, published on its own in the year *The Bridegroom* was written, 1825.

Page 52, line 25: *Guizot's new volume.* A single work by this historian and conservative politician of the post-Napoleonic era could run up to thirty volumes.

Page 53, lines 1, 2: *Béranger . . . Paër.* The songs of Pierre Jean de Béranger, voicing the aspirations of the Parisian working class, were hugely popular throughout Europe, including progressive circles in Russia, for much of the nineteenth century. Ferdinando Paër's forty-three operas include one, *Leonora*, that uses the same plot as Beethoven's *Fidelio.*

Page 53, lines 19–21: *Talma . . . Mamselle Mars . . . Potier.* Leading lights of the theater of the Napoleonic era. The Royalists circulated the legend that Talma gave Napoleon lessons in the conduct and manner of speech befitting an emperor.

Page 54, line 3: *God grant we'll soon be educated!* Not yet. Alexander I's educational policies centered on the eradication of "subversive, un-Russian" ideas and "free thinking." Staff of Russia's five universities were sacked for their ideas of constitutional government.

Page 54, line 9: *Moscow Telegraph.* A popular literary review that included a pictorial supplement showing foreign fashions in clothes, furniture, etc. Pushkin would resist efforts to get him to contribute, for he thought the magazine superficial. In one letter to a friend he gave his opinion of its editor: "The *Telegraph* fellow is decent and honest, but a fibber and an ignoramus . . ."

Page 61, line 3: *everything.* If Pushkin's work on the poem had run to a third morning he might have rhymed this line.

The Tale of the Dead Princess and the Seven Champions

Page 65, line 22: *She sighed the deepest sigh.* Pushkin's style in this folk tale abounds in diminutives, giving color and emphasis in various ways. Here, in language appropriate to a loved child's ears, *tyazhelò* ("heavy") is lengthened to five-syllable *tyazhel-yòshen'ko*, weightily taking up most of the line and enacting the sigh. This is typical of Pushkin, and especially in this poem.

Page 67, line 12: *towers.* Interpretation of Pushkin's word *terem* depends on the reader's architectural imagination. In early Russia, and in Russian legend and folk tale, the typical domestic dwelling took elevated form.

Page 70, line 22: *A tiled shelf on the stove.* A sleeping place on Russian stoves, used when the fire has died down but still emits warmth.

Page 72, line 9: *wine.* Literally "green wine," a term in folk poetry for vodka.

Page 76, line 24: *The little old woman.* Pushkin refines what is already a diminutive, *starùshka* ("little old woman"), by adding a syllable, *Starushònka.* Twelve lines further on, he dazzlingly adds yet another, *Starushònochka.* See note to page 65.

Page 83, line 20: *that deep cavern's entrance.* The deep *o* sounds of *Pòd goròyu tyòmnyy vkhòd* ("Beneath the mountain the dark entrance") convey the gaping entrance-hole of the cave.

Page 86, lines 12–13: *I was among the guests . . . scarcely wet.* The traditional Russian storyteller's standard closing lines, after which he will pass round the hat so as to be able to get his whiskers properly wet. Pushkin's verse folk tale *Tsar Saltan* ends with the same form of words.

The Tale of the Golden Cockerel

Page 89, line 14: *Men in thousands under arms.* Pushkin's "full line" here, consisting chiefly of a single monosyllable, *Mnoga-chìslennuyu rat',* is one of a number of two-word lines in *The*

Tale of the Golden Cockerel that contribute significantly to its slow, measured rhythm. These two-word lines have an incantatory quality, *Shamakhànskaya tsarìtsa* (or with its accusative *-uyu / u* ending) occurring three times.

Page 89, line 20: *west.* Here and elsewhere Pushkin has "east," which doesn't suit the rhyme in English so well. Russians I have discussed this with find no particular significance in this point of the compass; it is simply that the next attack comes from an unexpected direction.

Page 91, lines 5–6: *"Now Tsar ... / What an easy life for you!"* The words *Tsàrstvuy, lèzha nà boku!* ("Rule, lying on your side!") were removed by the censor on first journal publication. See also the last note below.

Page 93, lines 13–15: *Back and forth ... horses pass.* Pushkin deliberately slows the tempo. "The image of grass, red with blood," the critic Valentin Nepomnyashchy has written, "grows to a monstrous size in close-up ... in a narrative shorn of colorful adjectives" (*Soviet Literature*, No. 1, 1987, Moscow, p. 117). The mode of repetition is now set up for the tsar's ludicrous histrionics, in his own words and the next three lines of narrative.

Page 93, line 21: *groaned with grievous groan*: The repetition (see previous note) is in the original.

Page 93, lines 23–27: *Suddenly ... the Queen of Shamakhàn.* In four and a half lines Pushkin has twenty-two *a* sounds, seven of them in a single climactic line, making the whole passage, as it were, one long gasp: *Vdrug shatyòr / Raspakhnùlsya ... i devìtsa, / Shamakhànskaya tsarìtsa, / Vsya siyàya kak zaryà, / Tíkha vstrètila tsaryà.* I have thrown in *aw* along with *a* sounds, making a modest total compared to Pushkin's performance.

Page 94, line 14: *Charmed, enraptured.* These words take up one of Pushkin's full lines: "*Akaldòvan, vaskhishchòn.*"

Page 97, line 5: *Best not though, with some, insist.* A highly sensitive line. Pushkin first wrote "But with a mighty one it is bad to quarrel," changed this in his fair copy to "But with tsars it is bad to quarrel," and finally, before sending his manuscript to the censor, altered the line to (literally) "But with a certain one it is costly to quarrel." A reissue (1993) of B. V. Tomashevsky's one-volume edition of Pushkin's Complete Works, the "Golden Volume" (1935), restores the line as it was originally in the fair copy.

Page 97, lines 26–27: *This my tale ... our youth.* The censor, fearful of any possible political allusions, removed these lines too on first publication. (See the above note on the censor's removal of an earlier line.) Pushkin noted these cuts with indignation in his journal.

AFTERWORD: PUSHKIN'S VOICE IN ENGLISH

IT IS A common presumption among those who attempt metrical translations of Pushkin into English that his original verse forms should be kept at all costs. That Pushkin was a master of metrical schemes familiar in English tradition, which beckon to the translator, may well have strengthened the currency of this notion. One often sees an announcement, sometimes even on a title page, of Pushkin translated "in the prosodic forms of the original," as if that were a claim to authenticity. Of course, verse form can be a significant feature, more so in the case of narrative than of lyric verse. In narrative, the verse form takes on an especially strong flavor of its own – it would surely be unthinkable, for example, for a translator to change that of *Eugene Onegin*. In lyric verse, on the other hand, form and content are usually locked inextricably together in the original language; in other words, here form as well as content often has to be translated.

It has been insufficiently acknowledged that it is not always possible to match original verse forms in translation on a literary level. If the attempt is insisted upon, the resulting "translation" will be just as much of a mangle as if the entire content had been misconstrued. A key difference between the

Russian and the English languages lies in word length. Russian abounds in long sinuous words often extended by case and tense endings to five or six syllables; in English this number of syllables is rare except in abstract nouns, whereas monosyllables are frequent. So if both the metrical form and the number of lines of the original are kept, the translator must often introduce extra English words to make up for the syllabic shortfall, producing padding, circumlocution, and inflation, most un-Pushkinian qualities. And the constraints imposed by the need to maintain Pushkin's exact rhyme schemes commonly lead to unnatural English word order, such as a conveniently rhyming adjective following its noun.

I have managed broadly to keep Pushkin's original meter and rhyme scheme, however, in four of the five translations in this book by taking advantage of certain formal relaxations. I have not kept, for example, the regularly alternating masculine and feminine rhymes (with contrasting final stressed and weak syllable) customary in Russian verse, since the latter don't naturally occur with 50 percent frequency in English and often strike an unwanted satirical note. This has inevitably meant that some variety of cadence has been lost. Further, since rhyme is easier in Russian than in English, because of the frequency of similar-sounding inflected word-endings, I have considered it only fair to have occasional half and near rhyme in order to avoid the unpoetic contortions that pursuit of full rhyme would have involved.

Pushkin's favorite meter, the iambic tetrameter (ti-*tum* ti-*tum* ti-*tum* ti-*tum*[-ti]), perfectly fits the

Russian language, and the two strict formal examples of "narrative poems" in the present selection, *The Gypsies* and *Count Nulin*, are in this meter. Pushkin's polysyllables neatly and naturally occupy his line, which commonly has only three words, noun, verb, and adjective or adverb, and not infrequently only two. Russian words, however long, never take more than one stress; unstressed syllables fall lightly on the ear several at a time, and the Russian tetrameter, with four notional metrical stresses, usually ripples by with only two or three natural word stresses. Russian verse, and particularly Pushkin's, sounds more spontaneous and conversational than English, with its greater number of mono- and disyllables and hence greater proportion of stressed syllables. In pursuit of English speech rhythm I have allowed myself the freedom to chop a weak syllable from the beginning of a line (so changing an iambic line into a trochaic) and to reverse stress patterns (i.e., to have "*tum*-ti" instead of "ti-*tum*"), and I have occasionally thrown in an extra syllable (including ones the reader is invited to contract in speaking – "Whàt d(o) you sày?"). In English poetry these metrical freedoms are familiar. Furthermore, I have not attempted to be consistent in elision, and have scanned the same word, or the same kind of word, differently in different passages to suit the rhythm, which is often speech rhythm. For me the case for all this is confirmed by the experience of reading verse translations with impeccably regular scansion and rhyme: their effect, I find, tends to be self-conscious, self-satisfied, unengaged, and disembodied.

A final liberty I have taken – which I would say

isn't really a liberty at all – concerns the syllabic shortfall that takes place when Russian is translated literally into English. A striking example of the problem that faces the translator can be given from *Eugene Onegin*: "*Ostanovìlasya onà*," eight syllables, is one whole line of a tetrameter: "She stopped" in English. In the translations of non-stanzaic poems of continuous verse in this book broadly maintaining Pushkin's meter, I have accepted the syllabic shortfall, resulting in a reduced line count. My *Golden Cockerel*, for example, has about 7 percent fewer lines than the original. I see no other way of keeping up with the concentration of Pushkin's verse. However, unlikely as it might seem, it is possible to bring out original emphasis, word placement, repetition, verbal patterns, and even rhyme schemes, in verse translation even if overall contours change.

As for the ballad *The Bridegroom*, since Pushkin specifically chose the metrical form that he found in Bürger's ballad (see Introduction, page XXVII), it was *de rigueur* to adhere (in my way) to this exciting stanza form.

The metrical exception mentioned above among the translations in this book is *The Tale of the Dead Princess*. The meter of the original is trochaic tetrameter (a four-stress line starting with a stress) in rhyming couplets, Pushkin's favorite "folk" meter. Because of this poem's light and lucid texture – as compared, especially, to the dense *Golden Cockerel*, which is in the same meter – maximum freedom of expression was needed in translation if simplicity and spontaneity were at all to be achieved, and so, uniquely in this book, I have here evaded what would have been crippling metrical demands in English by departing from Pushkin's verse form, chopping the first, stressed, syllable of the line to produce a more manageable three-stress line (iambic trimeter), rhyming only every fourth line (occasionally more frequently); and as some compensation for the infrequency of rhyme, I have for once observed Pushkin's regular alternation of feminine and masculine line-endings. Only with such freedoms could I, I felt, have any hope of catching anything of the atmosphere and style of the original.

Pushkin's word-music, its physical basis the strong, highly colored, and dramatic sounds of Russian vowels and consonants, is of course often untranslatable; I have drawn attention in the endnotes to some unmatchable sounds. I have tried, however, to bring out the distinctive lexis, style, and register of each of Pushkin's poems. His *Gypsies* mingles Romantic with realistic language. *The Bridegroom* distills folk idiom. In *Count Nulin* the authorial voice is uppermost, not pressingly confidential as in *Eugene Onegin*, but knowing, gently detached and ironic, the language fizzingly *au courant*. *The Tale of the Dead Princess* has a folk-style directness and simplicity. *The Tale of the Golden Cockerel* uses slightly archaic folk language within a highly condensed and allusive narrative style. In diction I have generally aimed to bridge the gap between Pushkin's time and our own, and not to sound "period," too stridently of the current time, or of no time. Above all, I have sought stylistic unity, a voice, Pushkin's voice in English.

The Tale of the Golden Cockerel has always been popular with translators, and in recent years so has *Count Nulin*. There have been fewer attempts at *The Gypsies* and *The Bridegroom*, and fewer still at *The Tale of the Dead Princess*. Regardless of the number of previous translations, however, the rise of translation theory in recent decades has not been accompanied by the emergence of any substantial body of translation of Pushkin's verse that has impressed as verse in English; it is hard to think of any translation of Pushkin's poetry apart from *Eugene Onegin* that has caught on with the reading public or gained currency in non-specialist anthologies.*

Eugene Onegin has been pretty well translated by Charles Johnston (1977) and James Falen (1990), and Stanley Mitchell has an excellent version in preparation. Of Pushkin's other verse, however, worthwhile translations seem to have appeared only at rare moments since Pushkin's lifetime. From nineteenth-century translations I have seen I would single out George Borrow's unrhymed version of *The Gypsies*, done in Pushkin's lifetime, and William Lewis's *Fountain of Bakhchisaray*, which appeared a

* I find Maurice Baring's generally impressive translation of "The Prophet," which used to be much-quoted, spoiled by a last line that travesties Pushkin's meaning: God charges his prophet to "Lay waste with fire the heart of man." Baring's earlier prose version (in his introduction to *The Oxford Book of Russian Verse*, 1925) has, more to the point, "set light . . ."

dozen years after Pushkin's death; from the first half of the twentieth century, some translations of lyric poems by Donald MacAlister and Frances Cornford and a selection of lyric poems and dramatic verse by Vladimir Nabokov;* and from the second, versions of certain lyric poems by D. M. Thomas and Alan Myers, of single lyrics by Ted Hughes and Seamus Heaney, and of single narrative poems by Ranjit Bolt and A. D. P. Briggs.†

In his introduction to *The Oxford Book of Verse in English Translation* (1980), Charles Tomlinson explains that he has not included any versions of Pushkin, describing his typical experience of Push-

---

* In, respectively, George Borrow, *Works*, vol. 16 (London, 1924); *The Bakchesarian Fountain, by Alexander Pooshkeen; and other poems, by various authors*, translated by William D. Lewis (Philadelphia, 1849); *Echoes*, translated by Sir Donald Mac-Alister (Glasgow, 1923); *Poems from the Russian*, translated by Frances Cornford and Esther Polianowsky Salaman (London, 1943); and *Pushkin–Lermontov–Tyutchev: Poems*, translated by Vladimir Nabokov (London, 1947).

† In, respectively, *The Bronze Horseman: Selected Poems of Alexander Pushkin*, translated by D. M. Thomas (New York and London, 1982); *An Age Ago: A Selection of Nineteenth-Century Russian Poetry*, translated by Alan Myers (New York, 1988, and London, 1989); *After Pushkin: Versions of the Poems of A. S. Pushkin by contemporary poets*, edited by Elaine Feinstein (Manchester, 1999): "The Prophet" (Hughes), "Arion" (Heaney), "Tsar Nikita and His Daughters" (Bolt); and *Alexander Pushkin*, edited by A. D. P. Briggs (London, 1997): "The Bronze Horseman."

kin in English as being "rather staid but 'accurate' rendering into tame iambics." I agree with him (except for the word "accurate"), and in the translations in this book have done my best to redress the balance.

A. W.

ABOUT THE TRANSLATOR

ANTONY WOOD is a translator and publisher of European classic literature in translation. His other translations of Pushkin's poetry include the Little Tragedies (under the title *Mozart and Salieri*, Angel Books, London) and the original version of *Boris Godunov* (included in *The Uncensored "Boris Godunov"* by Chester Dunning and others, University of Wisconsin Press). He is a winner of the Max Hayward Award from the Translation Center at Columbia University, and in 1999, the bicentenary of Pushkin's birth, received a Pushkin Medal from the Russian government.

ABOUT THE ILLUSTRATOR

SIMON BRETT has been making wood engravings since 1961. His prints, bookplates, and book illustrations are among the finest of the present time, and he writes frequently on the history, practice, and current condition of the engraver's art.

A NOTE ON THE TYPE

THIS BOOK has been set in Garamond, a French Renaissance type with a noble heritage extending back to the types cut by Francesco Griffo for Aldus in the late 1400s. Chosen by Stanley Morison as one of the first types he revived for the Monotype Corporation, the roman was modeled after the types cut for Robert Estienne by Claude Garamond in Paris in the sixteenth century. At the time of the Monotype revival, Garamond had already become quite fashionable, appearing in the catalogues of most of the major typefoundries – though the success of those types depended heavily on the specimen followed in the recutting. ~ Claude Garamond is known to have cut only two italic types, neither of them as accomplished as his romans. As a result, the italic currently paired with Garamond is based on the types of Robert Granjon, one of the first French punchcutters to abandon the Italian preference for roman capitals with italic lowercase. As a pair the two types harmonize elegantly, displaying the "sparkle" so prized by typographers.

Design & composition by Carl W. Scarbrough